D0169769

THE *Fruit*
OF THE SPIRIT IS . . .
Patience

THE *Fruit*
OF THE SPIRIT IS...
Patience

A small group Bible study

Lynn Stanley

For the reader's convenience, the author cites verses from the King James *and* the New International Versions of the Bible. The translations appear side-by-side, with the NIV always appearing to the *left* of the KJV.

FOCUS
PUBLISHING, INC.
1375 Washington Avenue South
Bemidji, Minnesota 56601

THE *Fruit*
OF THE SPIRIT IS...
Patience

A Small Group Bible Study Series

Lynn Stanley

Copyright ©1999 by Focus Publishing
Bemidji, Minnesota 56601
All Rights Reserved

Scripture (KJV) taken for the The King James Version and (NIV) The Holy Bible, International Version©. Copyright © 1973, 1978, 1984 by the International Bible Society. Used by permission of Zondervan Publishing House.

ISBN 1-885904-18-5

Cover Art By Kathy Rusynck
Cover Design by Richard Schaefer

Printed in the United States of America

From the author...

Dear Reader:

The Holy Spirit of God is not an apparition: He is a Real Person who dwells in the hearts of all who believe on the Name of Jesus Christ (1 Corinthians 6:19), trust in Him as Savior (Ephesians 1:13), and follow the commandments of God (1 John 3:24). The author would be remiss in offering a study on the Fruits of the Holy Spirit, without first stressing the need for all who read it to be saved:

> ...*"I tell you the truth, no one can see the kingdom of God unless he is born again. ...No one can enter the kingdom of God unless he is born of water and the Spirit."*   *John 3:3, 5 (NIV)*

> ...*"The word is near you; it is in your mouth and in your heart," that is, the word of faith we are proclaiming: That if you confess with your mouth, "Jesus is Lord," and believe in your heart that God raised Him from the dead, you will be saved. For it is with your heart that you believe and are justified, and it is with your mouth that you confess and are saved.*   *Romans 10:8-10 (NIV)*

> *And you also were included in Christ when you heard the word of truth, the gospel of your salvation. Having believed, you were marked in Him with a seal, the promised Holy Spirit.*   *Ephesians 1:13 (NIV)*

All who desire to fully experience the supernatural power of God's Holy Spirit, must first confess their sins, being fully repentant and open to God's intervention in their lives. Second, they must believe that Jesus Christ died for their sins, was buried, rose from the dead, and lives today.

Respectfully,

Lynn Stanley

Introduction

We chose a watermelon for our cover because it is a good representation of the fruit of patience; those of us who love watermelon know that it requires some perseverance to eat it: Watermelons can be cumbersome and heavy, and are not easy to lift into the shopping cart. Watermelons are difficult to store because they are so large. They are difficult to cut, and (if you are lucky enough to find a really good one) they are *messy*. The seeds are troublesome and inconvenient, but once we take the time to separate them from the meat, we find that the sweet, juicy fruit was well worth the trouble. We would not have been able to enjoy the fruit without *patience*.

In this first in a series of studies on the Fruits of the Spirit, we thought it appropriate to begin with the topic of patience because patient perseverance is a staple of the Christian faith—a spiritual gift necessary for the acquisition of each of the other gifts. Neither love, joy, peace, kindness, goodness, faithfulness, gentleness *or* self-control, can be realized without *patience*. And without patient perseverance, we cannot receive the crown of life (James 1:12). As with each Spiritual fruit, patience grows only when it is nourished by Living Water. None of the Fruits of the Spirit are produced on our own; each is a gift of the Holy Spirit, grown out of an abiding faith in the Lord Jesus Christ. If saving faith in Jesus Christ is not accompanied by a desire to make Him Lord of your life, the fruits of God's Spirit will wither on your vine. If the sincere desire of your heart is to grow in the knowledge of Jesus Christ so that you may produce His fruit in order to feed a spiritually starved world, we are confident that God will use this study to encourage you.

Contents

pa·tience 1 : bearing pains or trials calmly or without complaint. **2** : manifesting forbearance under provocation or strain **3 :** not hasty or impetuous **4** : steadfast despite opposition, difficulty, or adversity **5** : able or willing to bear...
—-*Merriam Webster's Collegiate Dictionary,*
Tenth Edition

"Yet the Lord longs to be gracious to you; he rises to show you compassion. For the Lord is a God of justice. Blessed are all who wait for him!"
Isaiah 30:18

Chapter I

Why me?
Living With Adversity

Is it nothing to you, all who pass by?
Look around and see. Is any suffer-
ing like my suffering that was inflicted
on me, that the Lord brought on me
in the day of his fierce anger?
Lamentations 1:12 (NIV)

Scripture says the Lord sends rain upon the righteous and the unrighteous (Matthew 5:45) and Christians should not be surprised by suffering (1 Peter 4:12). God not only ordains some adversity, He actually tells
us to *rejoice* in it! Most of us can accept that truth intellectually, because
God has said it is so. But accepting that truth *in the heart* is an entirely
different matter.

At one time or another, all Christians struggle with the reality of
longsuffering. Sometimes we remind ourselves that we are God's children, and if God *really* loves us, it doesn't seem fair that we should suffer
just as those who do not follow Christ. Still, everyone who is reading this
may be suffering to some degree right now.

Some of us have suffered greatly in the past, and all of us will suffer
in the future. You or someone you love suffers physically. Some people
have financial problems. Some need a job, while others are suffering in
the job God gave them, working inside the home, or out in the world's
work force. Some people are suffering over a broken relationship, and
others struggle with defiant children, difficult marriages, or both. Many
people carry deep scars from wrongs suffered in the past. Sometimes we
suffer for friends and loved ones who don't know the Lord Jesus Christ
as Savior, and we know how much they need Him.

We have all had dreams that didn't come true and prayers that seem to go unanswered. Proverbs 14:10 tells us that each heart knows its own bitterness, and no one else can share its joy. Suffering is common to everyone, differing only in intensity with each individual. Knowing that suffering is inevitable, we must be prepared to endure if we plan to finish the race God has set before us (Hebrews 12:1). When it comes to the issue of long suffering, we have options: we can be consumed with trying to figure out the *reasons* for it, or we can make the better choice: we can take the focus off *ourselves,* and turn our eyes toward Jesus. *We can consciously choose to praise and thank Him, regardless of how things look or how we may feel.* In that way, adversity ceases to be a problem and becomes an opportunity in which to glorify God.

Read the book of Job. When he learned that all his children had perished, he tore his robe in anguish, fell on his face, and *worshipped* God (Job 1:21). In his wisdom, Job knew that God saw the *whole* picture, while he saw only a *portion* of it. Therefore, God's perspective was *very* different from his. Job was a holy man, blameless in God's sight. Scripture says two very important things about Job: he *knew God's promises,* and he *carried them in his heart.* In other words, he didn't just *know* Scripture, he *applied the truth* of God's word to his situation. As his circumstances grew worse, Job's spirit was nourished by the Word of God. God promises to rescue and restore those who trust in Him, and He always knows exactly how He is going to do it.

If you are pure and upright, even now he will rouse himself on your behalf and restore you to your rightful place.

Job 8:6 (NIV)

If thou wert pure and upright; surely now he would awake for thee, and make the habitation of thy righteousness prosperous.

(KJV)

So you handed them over to their enemies, who oppressed them. But when they were oppressed they cried out to you. From heaven you heard them, and in

Therefore thou deliveredst them into the hand of their enemies, who vexed them: and in the time of their trouble, when they cried unto thee, thou heardest them

your great compassion you gave them deliverers who rescued them from the hand of their enemies.
Nehemiah 9:27 (NIV)

from heaven; and according to thy manifold mercies thou gavest them saviours, who saved them out of the hand of their enemies. (KJV)

Knowing vs. Believing: Defining true faith

Christians will tell you that the ungodly suffer because of their disobedience—because they have rejected Christ. But what about those of us who have *surrendered* to Christ? Why do *we* suffer? The answer lies in the reality of the spiritual war between Satan and God's people, and *the outcome depends on whether or not the believer is willing to trust God and allow Him to work* in his life. The Christian who patiently perseveres through adversity is the one who enters the battle armed with the Word of God: he makes Scripture his weapon and God's righteousness his provision; he feeds on God's Word so that when the enemy strikes (and he will), he won't lack the spiritual energy to sustain his physical mind and body in battle.

For though we live in the world, we do not wage war as the world does. The weapons we fight with are not the weapons of the world. On the contrary, they have divine power to demolish strongholds.
2 Corinthians 10:4 (NIV)

For the weapons of our warfare are not carnal, but mighty through God to the pulling down of strong holds.   (KJV)

The victorious Christian not only perseveres *patiently* through affliction, he develops a stronger, deeper relationship with God because of it. As he grows spiritually, he understands that *God uses adversity to draw us nearer to Him.* In that way, the believer who loves God can *know* that *all adversity* will work for his/her *good!*

As we come to depend more upon God, He increases our faith. And as He increases our faith, we gain the strength—through His Holy Spirit—to persevere with patience. Simply put, *God uses pain to teach those who love Him,* and He is blessed when we trust Him enough to *view suffering as a gift* .

For it has been granted to you on behalf of Christ not only to believe on him, but also to suffer for him. *Philippians 1:29 (NIV)*	**For unto you it is given in the behalf of Christ, not only to believe on him, but also to suffer for his sake.** **(KJV)**

More than any other life experience, longsuffering exposes the character of the one who suffers. Suffering is like a mask: once it's pulled away, it reveals the *real* identity of the person behind it. Oswald Chambers said, "No man is the same after an agony, he is either better or worse."[1] Because of God's incredible grace, the Christian can emerge from *any* trial a better person, and a stronger witness for Jesus Christ.

Pain is a gauge by which God measures our trust in Him. But it isn't the magnitude of our suffering that He measures, it is our *reaction* to it. It is easy to trust God when things are going well, but those who continue to trust Him during adversity must surely please Him even more.

In addition to measuring our trust in God, pain and suffering are useful to Him for testing our spiritual agility. Problems are like hurdles on the tracks of our spiritual lives, and when those hurdles seem impossible to clear, those who *truly* trust in the Lord will find that His power is not only sufficient to lift them over, but it will allow them to *soar above* it.

Whatever the degree or form of pain, *God is able* to sustain us, *regardless of how impossible things look*. Patience and longsuffering are born of the faith that never quits—faith that *absolutely believes what God says*. When our *feelings* tell us that God can't help, *true faith* will hold our emotions in check. True faith won't allow *emotions* to obscure the *truth* of God's Word—truth that can be relied upon, regardless of how things look. *True faith* acknowledges the power and sovereign will of God in all things.

...we also rejoice in our sufferings, because we know that suffering produces perseverance; persever- ance, character; and character, hope. And hope does not disap- point us, because God has poured out his love into our hearts by the Holy Spirit, whom he has given us.   Romans 5:3-5 (NIV)

...we glory in tribulations also; knowing that tribulation worketh patience; And patience, experi- ence; and experience, hope: And hope maketh not ashamed; be- cause the love of God is shed abroad in our hearts by the Holy Ghost which is given unto us.   (KJV)

Because God does not lie, we can know *absolutely* that He will speak to us, comfort us, and rescue us in our suffering. We *know* that, because *God says so*! (Psalms 81:7 and 119:50) If our sincere desire is to experi- ence God's will in our lives, He *will* rescue us in *His* perfect time, and He will bless us in the midst of our suffering. He will restore us and make us strong, firm and steadfast. Once we learn to walk through the darkness by the light of faith, accepting God's word as inerrantly true, we develop the spiritual perseverance necessary to endure pain with dignity. True faith is the absolute knowing—-*without reservation*—- that God can be trusted to see us through the inevitabilities of life. Faith is like mother's milk, nurturing patience and perseverance in the believer. And when the battle is over, those who remain standing will be those who know God's Word and believe it.

And the words of the Lord are flawless, like silver refined in a furnace of clay, purified seven times.   Psalm 12:6 (NIV)

The words of the Lord are pure words: as silver tried in a furnace of earth, purified seven times.   (KJV)

Using Adversity to Glorify God

One of the most frustrating experiences of my life was learning to operate a computer. I was frustrated because I couldn't visualize how the computer worked. I couldn't concentrate on learning the functions of the keyboard because I was consumed with speculation over what a microchip was, and how it could have a memory better than mine! After several weeks, I finally decided that no matter how much I wanted to, I would never understand how computers work. In the same way, I don't understand how God works in my life, I only know that He does. God is sovereign, whether we understand Him or not. His judgments are unsearchable, His paths beyond tracing out. (Romans 11:33) It isn't necessary to see miracles in order to trust God because we know that *faith which is seen is not faith at all.*

But they do not know the thoughts of the Lord; they do not understand his plan, he who gathers them like sheaves to the threshing floor.
Micah 4:12 (NIV)

But they know not the thoughts of the Lord, neither understand they his counsel: for he shall gather them as the sheaves into the floor.
(KJV)

Other People's Pain

There are times when God may allow the believer to suffer because of other people's pain. For example, there are always consequences for sin, so when a child of God is involved in a relationship with an unbeliever, they may suffer because the unbeliever's sin directly affects them. Or, the relationship may be with a Christian who is consciously involved in sin, or a godly loved one who is suffering for reasons we don't understand. Whatever the reason, believers often suffer because of circumstances in the lives of other people.

One has to wonder what Mrs. Job was feeling as she observed her husband's suffering. There she was, married to "a blameless and upright man who feared God and shunned evil." They were wealthy, their children were many and healthy; life was *better* than a bowl of cherries! Then suddenly everything that could possibly go wrong, did. First, Job was attacked from all sides: he lost his animal herds and all but a few of his beloved servants died. Then a mighty wind swept down on the house where his children were gathered, killing all of them. While Job and his wife were still mourning the loss of their children, the Lord allowed Satan to afflict Job with painful sores from the top of his head to the soles of his feet. Can you imagine how Job's wife felt, seeing her husband like that? Can you even imagine how *she* was suffering? Job 19:17-20 says Job's breath was offensive to her, and that Job was a loathsome sight. It says he looked so disgusting that little boys scorned him and his intimate friends detested him; he was nothing but skin and bones.

I assume Mrs. Job was present when her husband's friends argued over the reason for his suffering. Later she probably listened as Elihu attempted to share with Job his opinion regarding God's redemptive purpose in affliction. When God shared the Divine perspective on suffering with Job, Job probably passed that insight on to his wife. But nowhere were Job or his wife given a logical reason for the suffering he *and his family* were forced to endure.

While God used affliction to teach even a blameless man like Job more about Himself, Mrs. Job just happened to be there. Sometimes that's the way it is. Sometimes we have to suffer because God is working in the life of someone else. When that happens, we're called to persevere with *patience*: to consider the other's suffering in an effort to learn what God desires to teach *us* through it, to exhort with gentleness and patience, and to *stay out of God's way*. And always, we must resist the temptation to hurry in and fix what God has allowed to be broken.

Recognize that when we pray for a loved one, God may use adversity to get their attention, and that will directly affect us. Be prepared for that. The spiritual dilemma is that we are inclined to want our loved ones to have good, happy lives. But the reality is that often people with good, happy lives don't see their need for God. Your prayers may bring an interruption to their lives.

Life Application: Chapter One

Day One:

What kind of man was Job, in God's eyes? Job 1:8

In spite of his righteousness, what kind of suffering did God allow in Job's life?

Job 1:14-17

Job 1:18

Carefully consider the degree and intensity of Job's suffering. How did Job feel? Job 6:1-4

Where was God while His servant suffered?

Day Two:
   Read and write notes on the following verses:

Job 31:6

Job 31:9-11

Job 31:16

Job 31:24

What can you see happening to Job in these passages?

Day Three:
   How does God teach us through suffering? Job 36:8-10

Job 33:14-18

Job 36:15

What gave Job the strength to persevere, in spite of his circumstances?

Describe the ways in which the strength of Job is available to all believers:

How will you apply this truth to your life? Discuss your answer with your group.

Day Four:

How did Job react during this time of excruciating emotional and physical pain?

Job 27:1-4

Job 27:11

Carefully consider Job's reaction. *As honestly as you can*, describe how you think *you* would react if God allowed even *some* of Job's adversity in your life:

Now record the way in which you think God *wants* you to respond:

Day Five:
Throughout Job's ordeal, God never addresses the question of divine justice, nor does He ever talk about Job's suffering. God neither condemns Job nor calls him innocent. In other words, God never answers Job's question, *"Why me, Lord? Why must I suffer like this?"* Why do you think that is? Read the following verses and paraphrase the scriptural answer.

Job 38:4

Job 40:2

Job 41:11

Record your understanding of suffering as it has been revealed to you in these Scriptures:

Read Job 38:1. When did God speak to Job?

Give an example of a time God "spoke" to you through your suffering and share with your group what God taught you.

What is the most significant thing God taught you through this lesson?

[1] Harry Verploegh, Editor, *Oswald Chambers The Best From All His Books*, (Nashville: Thomas Nelson Publishers, 1987), 345.

Chapter 2

Accepting God's Sovereignty

"In his heart a man plans his course,
but the Lord determines his steps."
Proverbs 16:9 (NIV)

The word *sovereignty* indicates supreme excellence and power. The God of the Bible is King of Kings and Lord of Lords. He was, is, and forever shall be. Because God's sovereignty is absolute, *absolutely nothing happens that He does not control.* And because God loves us, *everything He allows to happen will work toward our ultimate good.* With that knowledge we must *choose to trust Him.*

God is all-wise and exalted over all, and because He possesses unlimited wisdom and intelligence, He *always* knows what is best for us. Regardless of what we desire for ourselves, the simple truth is that there is no wisdom, no insight, no plan that can succeed against the Lord's will (Proverbs 21:30). To accept God's sovereignty is to acknowledge that He is *God Most High*—the *Absolute,* Supreme Ruler over all space and dominion.

...Then I praised the Most High; I honored and glorified him who lives forever. His dominion is an eternal dominion; his kingdom endures from generation to generation. All the peoples of the earth are regarded as nothing. He does as he pleases with the powers of heaven and the peoples of the earth. No one can hold back his hand or say to him: "What have you done?"

Daniel 4:34-35 (NIV)

...I blessed the most High, and I praised and honored him that liveth for ever, whose dominion is an everlasting dominion, and his kingdom is from generation to generation. And all the inhabitants of the earth are reputed as nothing: and he doeth according to his will in the army of heaven, and among the inhabitants of the earth: and none can stay his hand, or say unto him, What doest thou?

(KJV)

See now that I myself am He! There is no god besides me. I put to death and I bring to life, I have wounded and I will heal, and no one can deliver out of my hand.
Deuteronomy 32:39 (NIV)

See now that I, even I, am he, and there is no god with me: I kill, and I make alive; I wound, and I heal: neither is there any that can deliver out of my hand.
(KJV)

When we understand the truth about God's sovereignty, that truth becomes like strong arms that carry us through adversity. Once *head* knowledge becomes *heart* knowledge, adversity can be seen for what it is: an opportunity to *choose to believe what Scripture says, and then to rest in that choice and trust God for the outcome.* Romans 8:28 promises that God works *all* things together for the good of those who love Him. *Nothing happens to us or around us that has not been allowed by the God who loves us.*

Be joyful always; pray continually; give thanks in all circumstances, for this is God's will for you in Christ Jesus.
1 Thessalonians 5:16-18 (NIV)

Rejoice evermore. Pray without ceasing. In every thing give thanks: for this is the will of God in Christ Jesus concerning you.
(KJV)

Remember the story of Joseph? His brothers were jealous of him so they sold him into slavery and then convinced their father that Joseph was dead. Later Joseph was falsely imprisoned. Joseph didn't know God's ultimate plan for his life, yet he continued to praise God in spite of the suffering and unjust persecution he received for much of his life. When Joseph's long ordeal finally ended, he said to his brothers: *"And now, do not be distressed and do not be angry with yourselves for selling me here, because it was to save lives that God sent me ahead of you...So then, it was not you who sent me here, but God... You intended to harm me, but God intended it for good to accomplish what is now being done, the saving of many lives."* (Genesis 45:5, 8 and 50:20) Though God used mortal men to accomplish His Divine purpose in Joseph's life, Joseph knew that it was God Most High who allowed and controlled his suffering. And while Joseph was suffering, God gave him the grace to remember that His love is perfect. Man's knowledge and wisdom are limited, but the knowledge and wisdom of the Sovereign God are infinite. While it is possible for believers to gain godly wisdom through Scripture, *Divine* wisdom—wisdom that knows what is best from beginning to end—belongs to God alone.

But the plans of the LORD stand firm forever, the purposes of his heart through all generations.
Psalm 33:11 (NIV)

The counsel of the Lord standeth for ever, the thought of his heart to all generations.
(KJV)

Many are the plans in a man's heart, but it is the LORD'S purpose that prevails.
Proverbs 19:21 (NIV)

There are many devices in a man's heart; nevertheless the counsel of the Lord, that shall stand.
(KJV)

Suffering is never a mistake because *God's way is perfect.* Everything that happens—past, present and future—is allowed so that God's eternal purpose can be established in our lives. Our recognition of God's sovereignty compels us to *make a choice to trust Him,* one event at a time. To those who remain joyful in hope, patient in affliction and faithful in prayer, God's reward is a peaceful heart in the midst of turmoil. The peace God gives allows us the presence of mind to *stay focused on the only thing that really matters: our relationship with Jesus Christ.* Because we know that God loves us and that nothing happens apart from His will, we can have complete assurance that He can be trusted to know what is best for us.

God's Point of View

"For my thoughts are not your thoughts, neither are your ways my ways," declares the Lord. "As the heavens are higher than the

For my thoughts are not your thoughts, neither are your ways my ways, saith the Lord. For as the heavens are higher than the earth, so are my ways higher than your ways and my thoughts than your thoughts." Isaiah 55:8-9 (NIV)

earth, so are my ways higher than your ways, and my thoughts than your thoughts. (KJV)

God created us with an innate curiosity. To ask "why?" is natural for man, but to brood over hardship is a sin. Too much time spent searching for reasons takes time away from prayer, and the devil will use our curiosity to distract us from learning what God is trying to teach us. It is all right to ask God to reveal His reasons to you, but if He doesn't, let it go. God doesn't owe us any explanations. A. W. Tozer wrote the following regarding salvation; I believe it applies to suffering as well: "...We shall not seek to understand in order that we may believe, but to believe in order that we may understand. The idea of God as infinitely wise is at the root of all truth. It is a datum of belief necessary to the soundness of all other beliefs about God."[1]

Because God knows everything about us, His knowledge of our pain is personal and compassionate. He created our inmost being and knit us together in our mother's womb. God knows our physical and emotional limits, and He knows every detail of our lives. He has perfect knowledge and understanding of His creation. Certainly He knows what is best for us.

How many are your works, O Lord! In wisdom you made them all... Psalm 104:24 (NIV)

It was good for me to be afflicted so that I might learn your decrees. Psalm 119:71

O Lord, how manifold are thy works! in wisdom hast thou made them all: the earth is full of thy riches. It is good for me that I have been afflicted; that I might learn thy statutes." (KJV)

We can know the will of God as it is revealed through Scripture, but we can't know the intention of God, nor can we always determine His reasons. If we submit to God, we can gain wisdom and spiritual insight through suffering, even though we may never understand the "why" of it. If our desire is to learn from God, His wisdom will become a lifeline, hoisting us from the pit of adversity.

God's Providence

Providence means that God intervenes in our affairs: He controls the circumstances in our lives so that specific results will occur. From the human perspective, both good and bad things happen as a result of God's providence. From the *Divine* perspective, God allows *nothing* that is not for our ultimate good (Romans 8:28).

A common response to suffering is to blame someone else. We do this partly out of a need to find a reason for the pain, and partly because we don't want to accept responsibility for our own sin—sin which could actually have caused the pain we are suffering. It would have been easy for Joseph to blame his brothers, to hate them for the pain they had caused him. But instead, Joseph *chose* to acknowledge God's providence in his life.

God's ultimate goal in all providence is to glorify Himself and accomplish good for His people. Since nothing happens apart from God's will, no one can frustrate your plans or bring calamity to your house apart from willingness of God to allow it. Remember: Satan needs permission to touch God's people (Job 1:12, 2:6). We may find it difficult to believe when we're hurting, but the same God who allows us to suffer, rejoices in doing us good (Jeremiah 32:41).

When calamity comes, go to God in prayer and ask for the grace to praise Him in spite of it. We don't have to dread suffering. Instead, we can choose to see it as an opportunity to test God's faithfulness. In other words, we can make a *conscious choice* to submit to the inevitable and rest in God's promise to deliver us. We can *choose* to wait patiently for His intervention on our behalf. *Trust Him.* Things are never too tough for God! Though the world may throw us into a blazing furnace, the God we serve *promises* to rescue us (Daniel 3:17). We must stop worrying about *how* He's going to do it, and simply let him *do* it!

Man's Timing vs. God's Timing

When we hurt the most, we are called to wait in faith and rest in the assurance that God is in *complete* control. As we wait patiently for Him to act, we must pray for His sustaining grace, and ask for the wisdom to see things from His point of view. Instead of asking, *"Why me?"* we can *listen,* and always learn something significant from God. As we pray and wait for God's Spirit to move us toward holiness, we can choose to give Him glory for what He is about to do in our lives, and in the lives of those we love. Not only is it *possible* to give God thanks and praise for our suffering, it is *commanded* in Scripture (1 Thessalonians 5:16-18). When we choose to obey what God tells us through His word, His grace will abound to us.

It is not difficult to understand our impatience with God. Our society has a microwave mind set: We think, if it can't be done right away, it's not worth the trouble. We eat in fast food restaurants and get our cars serviced at places called "Jiffy Lube" and "Minute Man". Express and over-night delivery aren't fast enough anymore; we can fax things in a matter of minutes. We use one-hour dry cleaners and Photomats, and we get upset if we can't get a new pair of glasses in less than a day. We can fly from New York City to London, England in eight hours, and read a couple of condensed novels on the way.

For a thousand years in your sight are like a day that has just gone by...   Psalm 90:4 (NIV)

For a thousand years in thy sight are but as yesterday when it is past, and as a watch in the night. (KJV)

God has promised that if we call on Him, He will answer our prayers (Psalm 55:19). If God is making us wait for an answer, there is a reason. We may not be spiritually ready to receive that which we desire. It is also possible that the thing we're praying for is not God's will for us at all, in which case He'll probably *never* allow us to have it. Remember: God sees the *whole* picture, while we only see *part* of it. God wrote your story, and He knows how it will end. God makes us wait for lots of different reasons. If you are certain that what you're praying for is in accord with His will, you must persevere in prayer no matter how long it takes. *Pray without ceasing.*

Sometimes we wait, thinking the pain will never end. That's when we have to remind each other that *for the believer, all pain is temporary,* regardless of it's kind or intensity. Sometimes Christians must wait so that when the answer comes, God will receive all the glory. Mary and Martha sent for Jesus to come and heal their brother, Lazarus, who was sick. Scripture records that Jesus loved these friends, yet He delayed His coming and Lazarus died (Luke 11:1-44). The delay ultimately brought greater glory to God, when Lazarus was raised for the dead.

And the God of all grace, who called you to his eternal glory in Christ, after you have suffered a little while, will himself restore you and make you strong, firm and steadfast. 1 Peter 5:10 (NIV)	*But the God of all grace, who hath called us unto his eternal glory by Christ Jesus, after that ye have suffered a while, make you perfect, stablish, strengthen, settle you.* *(KJV)*

If things look hopeless, it is probably because we fail to look past the temporal. The world in which we live embraces values that are in opposition to the values of God. We are, in fact, a nation which has completely turned it's back on God. If this world was all God offered us, wouldn't it be difficult to believe He loved us? That is why it is so important to set our eyes and hearts on *eternity.* When we get our focus back on Jesus and all God has promised through faith in Him, we can look forward to eternity and the hope of eternal life with Christ. Even though the human mind can't fully comprehend the bliss which exists in the heavenly realm, the hope of heaven will sustain us during suffering because that is a promise of God.

Now we see but a poor reflection as in a mirror; then we shall see face to face. Now I know in part; then I shall know fully, even as I am fully known. *1 Corinthians 13:12 (NIV)*	*For now we see through a glass, darkly; but then face to face: now I know in part; but then shall I know even as also I am known.* *(KJV)*

If we were capable of understanding the joy that awaits us in heaven, we would view pain in relation to that indescribable joy, and it would seem insignificant by comparison. And we can *hope in what is to come,* as we trust God and choose to live by faith, not by sight:

...No eye has seen, no ear has heard, no mind has conceived what God has prepared for those who love him. 1 Corinthians 2:9 (NIV)

...Eye hath not seen, nor ear heard, neither have entered into the heart of man, the things which God hath prepared for them that love him. (KJV)

If we believe God brings good out of *all* things for those who love Him, we can be joyful in affliction, knowing that pain is always beneficial, and always used to urge us toward perfection (Isaiah 38:17, Hebrews 2:10). *All adversity exists under God's control.* Once we acknowledge that fact and submit to it, God will use all suffering to teach us more about Himself.

The circumstances of life include suffering, and suffering takes place during a period of time. How do you spend that time? Are you teachable? Is it your desire to make the most of a bad situation and use adverse circumstances to grow in your walk with the Lord? Are you ridden with anxiety, or can you rest in God's complete sovereignty, knowing that His plan cannot be thwarted? Can you ask God for the grace to accept what is, and what is to come?

Life Application: Chapter Two

Day One:

Look up the following verses and record what each says about the character of God:

Exodus 34:6-7

Deuteronomy 32:4

Psalm 139:1-4

Think carefully about God's attributes. Why can He be trusted to know what is best for those who love Him?

Day Two:

Read Jeremiah 29:11-13. Why does God desire the best for His children? (v.12-13)

What does it mean to you, to know that God desires the best for you?

What does Hebrews 12:7-8 tell you about adversity?

Read Job 1:8-12. What do verses 9-11 say about Satan and the way in which he works?

What do verses 10 and 12 say regarding God's protection of His people and His control over adversity?

Day Three:

Read Job 2:10. When Job's wife lost all hope, what was his response to her?

Why do you think Job responded as he did?

Read Isaiah 45:5-7 and record your understanding of God's sovereignty:

What does God's sovereignty mean to you, personally?

In what specific ways does God speak to us through our suffering?

Job 36:15-16

Isaiah 38:17

Philippians 1:29

What does it mean, to have something "granted" to you?

What was the last gift you received, and how did you feel when it was given to you?

Why do you think God allows believers to suffer?

Day Four:
Read Hebrews 12:10-11. Record the benefits of suffering:

Record a specific experience in which God used suffering to your benefit:

What is the most significant thing you learned, as a result of that trial?

Day Five:
In summary of this chapter, re-read the Scripture verses (printed in italics) within it's text. *Using just one or two words for each verse*, note the truth in each that is most meaningful to you.

Which of the verses that you read this week has made the most significant difference in your life? Discuss your answer within your group.

[1] A. W. Tozer, *Knowledge of the Holy,* (San Francisco: Harper & Row Publishers, 1961), pp. 59- 60.

Chapter 3

A Ready Defense

*"The weapons we fight with are not the
weapons of the world. On the contrary,
they have divine power to demolish
strongholds. We demolish arguments
and every pretension that sets itself up
against the knowledge of God, and we
take captive every thought to make it
obedient to Christ."*
2 Corinthians 10:4-5 (NIV)

An attribute is a *quality* —a characteristic that identifies a person
and often sets him apart from others. In order to know God intimately,
one must study His Word carefully and consider—-*in context*—everything God says about Himself. Once, I attempted to keep a running list
of the attributes of God. I kept a piece of notebook paper in my Bible and
listed the characteristics of God as they were revealed throughout Scripture. Some verses would identify Him specifically: *God Most High, Holy
One of Israel, Redeemer*, etc.. Others would come to me when I read
about something God did that revealed His character. For example,
Deuteronomy 20 begins with God telling the Jewish people not to be
afraid if they enter battle and their enemies are better prepared; He promises to be with them. He tells them that before the battle begins, the priest
will address the army and He even tells them what the priest will say.
Then God tells the Hebrews that they will win the battle. From that one
fraction of Scripture, I noted the following truths about God:

1. God is **omniscient**; He knows everything. He knew His people were
   going into battle even before they did, and He knew the enemy would
   have the advantage.

2. God is **personal**; He is our God. He refers to Himself as the "Lord your God."
3. God is **all-powerful**; His strength and ability are immeasurable. He brought His people out of slavery and He will deliver them safely from battle.
4. God is **faithful**; He does what He promises.
5. God is **trustworthy**; He won't desert His people.
6. God is **sovereign**. He was in control of every detail of this situation, right down to the exact words the priest would speak. In the same way, He controls the life of every believer.
7. God is **omnipresent**; He is everywhere, all the time.
8. God is **dependable**; He fights for us.
9. God is the **Great Protector**.
10. God is our **Peace**. We need not worry; we needn't give way to panic or anxiety.
11. God is our **Provider.** He gave His people what they needed to fight the battle, and he continually provided their daily needs.
12. God is the **Sustainer of all life**.
13. God is **victorious**, and promises victory to those who stay close to Him.

From three verses of Scripture, I learned *thirteen* truths about God; Bible scholars could probably find more. You can see why, after several weeks of continually adding adjectives to my list, I determined that it is probably impossible to list them all.

When considering God's character, one must understand that all of God's attributes are part of One Perfect Whole—though each attribute can (and should) be considered individually, none can be separated, one from the other. For example, it is impossible to understand God's forgiveness if you don't understand His mercy. And you cannot understand God's mercy without understanding His judgment. Judgment cannot be understood apart from an understanding of God's righteousness, and the concept of righteousness means nothing if one doesn't understand God's pure moral nature.

During times of adversity, one of the first things we do is question God's character: If God is love, why am I suffering? (We are questioning

His perfect love and wisdom.) If God is so merciful, why doesn't He show that mercy now? Why doesn't He deliver me from this awful circumstance? (We are questioning His compassion, His power and His ability.) When we hurt the most, when we feel trapped and can see no way out, *God's perfect sovereignty is the attribute which must be remembered above all the others.*

⟶►●◄⟵

The week after Donna and Dick's thirty-first wedding anniversary, Dick told his wife he was leaving her. "I don't love you anymore," he said. "...I haven't loved you for a long time."

"I knew he wasn't happy," Donna admitted, "...but I never thought he'd *leave!* Marriages have ups and downs all the time but you don't just *leave* after thirty-one years! No marriage is perfect, but I thought ours was really close. I *loved* being married. Taking care of Dick and the children was all I ever wanted to do—and I was *good* at it, too; Dick always went out of his way to say so....

"I still don't understand why he left and I probably never will," she continued. "Once he made up his mind there was no changing it; he left, and that was it.

"When Dick left, *everything* changed. We had raised five children *together.* Suddenly they were all *gone,* and so was he. For the first time in thirty-one years, I was completely alone. To say I was devastated is an understatement. I depended on Dick for everything. He was my most intimate friend. He was my *partner* and I expected to grow old with him. After all, we both said vows before *God!* Surely—-I thought—-he wouldn't go through with a divorce! He'd leave for a while, realize what a great life we had together, and come back.... That's what I *thought*, but of course that's not what happened.

"I used to think God was punishing me. I turned a multitude of sins over in my mind, trying to determine which of them had finally caused God to allow the destruction of my marriage. It took a long time for me to realize how *foolish* those thoughts were. It isn't God's will for *any* marriage to fail. Marriages fail because *human beings* fail. We are selfish and self-absorbed and sometimes too lazy to expend the energy that it takes to work things out. Dick *refused* to seek counsel from our pastor or anyone else. He refused to talk about any of it. He just *left*!

"Before and throughout the divorce proceedings, and since my marriage ended, God's Word has been the *one* constant in my life. I read Scripture the first thing every morning and I try to read each night before I go to sleep. God's Word sustains me. From the beginning, He gave me the wisdom to see that He is Sovereign in *all* things—not just in *good* things. He has shown me time and again how important it is to depend upon *Him* for the very things I used to rely on Dick for: intimacy, strength, provision, counsel...*friendship*. I'm still standing," she said, smiling. "My children and grandchildren, and my activities at church keep my life full and wonderful. My life isn't better or worse than it was when I was married; it's just *different*. I know *now* that my God is All Sufficient! He is everything I need...."

"It would be nice," she added, "...if we could understand Truth like that without suffering, but most of us can't."

Donna chose to rely on God during the worst adversity of her life. By reading Scripture daily, she demonstrated how the more one comes to know God in an intimate way, the less one questions the adversity He allows. *God does what He does because He is God!* He allows what He allows because He is the sovereign, all-wise Lord of the universe —the Ruler over all creation. *Once we truly believe in our hearts everything that God tells us about Himself*—-that He is merciful and just, with grace sufficient for *all* circumstances—we will stop trying to decipher His motives and continue to glorify His Name, even when we hurt. We will begin to live as the apostle Paul did: We'll stop sniveling and begin to consider it a *privilege* to share in the sufferings of Christ.

Paul was overwhelmed by what he owed Christ for His ultimate sacrifice on the cross. In 2 Corinthians 12:15, Paul said, *"I will very gladly spend for you everything I have and expend myself as well."* You see, Paul knew that *nothing* he would suffer—including death—could compare to the sacrifice Jesus made for his sake, and for the sake of all who would believe. From prison and in chains, under fear of death, Paul said,

"I will continue to rejoice...and hope that I will in no way be ashamed, but will have sufficient courage so that now as always Christ will be exalted in my body, whether by life or by death" (Philippians 1:20).

All human suffering must be measured against the cross.

Our Weapons In Battle

Though our battles with adversity are natural, the weapons with which we fight are *super*natural. From the human perspective, entering into suffering without a mature knowledge of God's Word is like entering battle without benefit of a weapon. We use God's Word as a bullet-proof shield; it will keep us from being destroyed as long as we hold it in front of us.

When Jesus was ready to begin His ministry, He was forced to stand in the desert, face-to-face with the greatest adversary of all. Armed only with the Word of God, Jesus held the enemy at bay during forty days and nights of unrelenting deprivation. Throughout His testing, Jesus held tightly to the promises of God.

During the lifetime of Jesus, the Jewish people had a saying: "The Holy One, blest be His name, does not elevate a man to dignity until he has first tried and searched him; if he stands in temptation then he raises him to dignity."[1] Because Jesus was a human being, it was necessary for God to test Him. When tempted by the devil, *Jesus made a choice of His own free will to follow God.* Likewise, God tests the rest of us for the same reason. We must make a lot of choices when we suffer: Will we pray or complain? Will we submit or sin? Will we wait on the Lord, or run ahead?

The testing of Jesus, as told in Matthew four, does not give a lot of detail regarding Christ's suffering, but we know He went without food for forty days (v.2). Scripture doesn't tell us exactly where the tempta-tion took place, but historians assume it was somewhere between the Jordan River (where Jesus had just been baptized) and Jerusalem. The area, located about thirty miles outside of the city, is quite barren and the landscape jagged and warped. The Dead Sea lies just to the south and because it is the lowest spot on earth, the heat can be intense. Jesus hadn't eaten for forty days, and at best we know He was extremely uncomfortable.

Satan took advantage of the Lord's weak physical state to tempt Him in three ways: First, he tempted Jesus to use His power selfishly. Next, Satan suggested that Jesus magnify Himself by presenting Himself to the multitudes as a miracle-worker. Finally, the devil tried to convince Jesus that *his* way was better than God's—that Jesus could "have it all" without suffering the pain of the cross. To this Jesus responded, *"Away from me Satan! For it is written, 'Worship the Lord your God, and serve Him only"* (v.10).

At this point, the importance of memorizing Scripture cannot be overstated: *The Word of God was the only weapon Jesus had to defend Himself against sin.* When one is engaged in a spiritual battle, having a Bible but not *knowing* Scripture is akin to having a pistol with no bullets.

A most significant truth is found in the verse immediately following the Lord's direct confrontation with the adversary: *"Then the devil left him, and angels came and attended him."*

Can't you just hear Jesus' sigh of relief, once it was over? Can't you just see Him, sitting exhausted on a flat rock somewhere out in the wilderness, all alone with God? He breathes deeply, His nostrils filling with the sweet smell of wildflowers growing in the desert. He rests His head back and casts weary eyes toward heaven. The only sounds He hears are the lonesome cooing of a dove, and the rustling of angel's wings as they eagerly attend the Son of God. All the beauty of God's creation surrounds Jesus, bringing peace to His tired soul as He realizes that *it is finally over....*

As happens to all of us sooner or later, Jesus was put to the test. After He stood firm, claiming the promises of God as His defense, a merciful and gracious God restored Him by sending a host of heavenly angels to care for Him. God will do the same for us.

The testing in the desert was the first of recorded sufferings in the life of Christ. It was the skirmish that helped to prepare Him for His greatest battle: the cross. The test in the wilderness, which would pale by comparison to the ultimate test at Calvary, proved Christ's mettle and set a precedent for the rest of us to follow: No one will escape the crosses of life. If we can't survive the battles, we can never win the war!

Life Application: Chapter Three

Day One:
Find the following verses and record what each says about the character of God:

1 Samuel 2:6-7

1 Chronicles 29:11-12

Hebrews 13:8

Daniel 9:9

Psalm 139:10

Review your notes. What do these verses teach about suffering and patience?

Day Two:
Study each verse in Psalm 66:8-12 and record your thoughts on adversity:

What did the people do? v.8

Why were they praising God? v.9-10

What kinds of adversity did God save them from? v. 11-12

Where did they find themselves when the trials were over? v.12

Record a specific way in which God refined you (made you more like Jesus) through adversity.

Day Three:

Read Psalm 139:23-24. If you have made these verses your prayer, ask God to reveal to you any sin in your life that may be contributing to the adversity you face right now. Record your thoughts. *If you feel comfortable*, share your insight with your group.

Why is it necessary for man to ask God to reveal sin in his life?

Jeremiah 17:9

Proverbs 16:2

Why is it possible to be in sin and not know it?

Day Four:

Read Romans 8:35-39. Based upon these verses, and considering all that you have learned about the attributes of God, where do you think God is, and how do you think He feels when you are suffering?

What does that truth mean to you?

Day Five:

Why is it important to *know* Scripture?

What are some of the things you do to stay disciplined in the study of God's Word?

Describe a specific time that you claimed one of the promises of God during adversity, and He delivered you.

[1] William Barclay, *The Gospel of Matthew,* (Edinburgh: St. Andrew Press), 1963, Volume 1, p. 56.

Chapter 4

An Imitation of Christ

*"Not only so, but we also rejoice in
our sufferings, because we know that
suffering produces perseverance."*
Romans 5:3 (NIV)

I once had a creative writing professor who would pound her fist on her desk and shout, "Don't *tell* me; *show* me!" That has proven to be the most useful advice I've ever received pertaining to writing fiction. The best stories ever written *show* the reader the emotions of the main characters instead of simply *telling* the reader what the people are feeling. One of the finest examples of "Don't tell me, show me," is found in the Bible:

And being in anguish, he prayed more earnestly, and his sweat was like drops of blood falling to the ground. **Luke 22:44 (NIV)**

And being in an agony he prayed more earnestly: and his sweat was as it were great drops of blood falling down to the ground. **(KJV)**

In that example, Luke does not have to *tell* the reader about the deep emotion Jesus was feeling; he has *shown* us by describing *sweat, like drops of blood....*

I have witnessed much pain and suffering in the Christian community. Christian marriages *do* fall apart, and Christians *do* lose loved ones. They can lose their jobs just as non-believers do, and many suffer financially. Even Christians must deal with problems of drug abuse and illegitimacy, and Christianity does not insure safety from violent crime or freedom from illness. To be sure, faith in Jesus Christ docs not give the believer immunity from suffering. But as painful as such experiences are, I have yet to see anyone suffer enough to sweat blood—to suffer as Jesus did.

The command, *"Don't tell me, show me,"* though most helpful in developing creative writing skills, is even more appropriate when applied to the Christian life. Christians are always being observed by the world—even more closely in times of affliction. Everyone, believers and non-believers alike, knows a "Christian" who tells off-color jokes, drinks to excess, or cheats and lies. Some even steal and commit adultery. You may know of at least one Christian who gave in to adversity and turned away from the Lord. Maybe the turning away was temporary, but it was a turning away, nonetheless. If you have turned away or know someone who has, you may have forgotten that suffering is allowed for our benefit.

Scripture says suffering for the sake of the Gospel has been *"granted to us."* (Philippians 1:29) The word, "granted" translates from the Greek, "charizomai," and signifies *a show of favoritism.* The verb means to give freely—to *bestow upon* someone, as a valuable gift.

For a moment, consider how you would react if you received an unexpected gift. You arrive home after a hard day's work and there it is, on the kitchen table: An old wooden box, about the size of your mother's jewelry box but not nearly as elegant looking. It is made of wood, but warped and chipped and covered with dust. Actually, it looks so ugly you don't even want to pick it up. There's a card propped against it, with your name scrawled clearly on the envelope. You open it and read the following: *"This is for you. With love, from Uncle Dudley."*

Staring at the dusty, chipped old box, you tell yourself not to be disappointed. You knew your uncle wasn't wealthy. And your mother always taught you that it's the *thought* that counts. Still, this thing is pretty ugly. Try as you may, you are unable to feel much gratitude, so you toss the card on the table, wondering where you can hide it until Uncle Dud comes to visit.

Returning later to the table you look again at the box and lift the lid. When you see what's inside, you can't believe your eyes; this was *totally* unexpected! The battered, dirty, ugly looking box is full of precious stones! You jump up, your fingers plunging into the box like ten greedy divers into an oyster bed. For a moment, time stands still. *You're rich!*

After awhile, you calm down and start pulling out the precious stones, examining them one-by-one: Diamonds... emeralds... rubies... sapphires. A few garnets, but they're not worth as much.... Each is unique, each is valuable. After examining your treasures you are astonished by the fact that something could look so bad at first glance, and have so much value.

Suffering is just like that. It looks pretty bad from the outside, but if you're willing to take a closer look, you can see the value of it. *Intimacy with God is the crown jewel of suffering*, the diamond of absolute assurance that we receive when we fully understand that we can trust Him. The more we lean on God, the more closely we feel His presence and the more real He becomes to us.

After the crown jewel, come emeralds of insight and wisdom as God reveals Himself more fully to us. As we pray and listen for God, we will recognize the peace that surpasses all understanding: the comfort of God's Holy Spirit. As we wait patiently for God to rescue us, He will reveal more about His love, His mercy, and His awesome power. Each revelation—whether new or freshly acknowledged by us—will add one more jewel to the crown of our faith.

If we stay near to God during difficult times, we emerge from our suffering with important revelations about ourselves and others—these are the rubies. The garnets of adversity are the little, less important things we learn to help us cope with the "big" things. Suffering is an ugly box which, if accepted with gratitude, will become a treasure chest transforming our faith into a valuable personal possession.

We suffer for various reasons. We suffer because God's ultimate goal is to bring everyone to Himself. Because He loves us, He may allow pain in our lives. If so, He has determined that it is the way to accomplish His objective, which is to make us conformed to the image of Christ (Romans 8:18-30). Remember: God didn't spare His own Son. Why should He spare us?

Paul's greatest desire in Philippians 3:10 is *"...that I may know him...and the fellowship of his sufferings."* Paul's desire was that when suffering came, he would react to, respond to, and endure it *as Jesus would*. Remember *in the flesh*, even Jesus pleaded, *"would that this cup* be taken from me...even so...thy will be done."

If we *choose* to rejoice during adversity, we are obeying the Lord's command to "give thanks in all things" and because of our obedience, God will be glorified through our suffering. For that, we can be *truly* thankful.

Bella was bent over her desk, too busy to notice the two policemen behind her, talking to her boss. When she noticed her co-workers staring at her, she turned to look—-just as her boss pointed toward her desk. Surprised, she looked back at her co-workers, and then to her boss. Raising her eyebrows curiously, she pointed a finger at herself: *"Me?"* she asked.

When her boss gave a slow affirmative nod, she knew something was wrong. *Terribly* wrong. Hesitant, she slid her chair away from her desk, stood up, and walked toward the men.

While her co-workers strained to hear the conversation, one officer began to speak softly. He was trying to look at Bella as he spoke, but it was obvious to the onlookers that he was having a difficult time: His eyes shifted to the floor briefly, but then he looked directly at Bella and told her—in the most gentle way he could—-that her only son had just been found dead from a self-inflicted gunshot wound.

Bella's hands flew up to cover her mouth —-an effort to stifle the scream she felt inside. But there was no scream. Only silence. And then, softly, the sound of her co-worker's voice: *"Oh, my God, NO!"* She ran to Bella's side, wanting to throw her arms around her and comfort her, but Bella stood frozen, unable to move. Then after a moment, she took a deep breath, straightened herself, and said the first thing that came into her mind: *"The Lord gives and the Lord takes away. Blessed be the Name of the Lord forever."*

"I really believe that," she says years later. "I believed it then, and I believe it now. God gives and God takes away. I can't explain the peace that came over me when I said those words. The people in the office said

I fainted, but I think the Lord just put me to sleep because He knew I needed to be rested for what lay ahead. Suicide is a devastating thing. It leaves the rest of us with the guilt of wondering what we should have done differently. For a long time, I felt as if it was my fault because when Ricky came back from Viet Nam I *knew* he wasn't the same as when he left. I *knew* something was wrong but he wouldn't talk to me. He kept telling us he wasn't taking drugs, but I knew he was. That's why we made him move out of the house. Then after he killed himself, my husband said maybe he wouldn't have done it if we had let him stay home. But it wouldn't have been right to let him live in our house *knowing* that he was using drugs; that would be like telling him we didn't care!"

There is passion in her voice: "But I *did* care! I loved my boy enough to suffer the misery of making him live on the street if that's what it would take for him to get off the drugs. I loved him enough to lay awake nights praying for him...."

"After a suicide, everyone looks for someone else to blame. But no one is to blame; *Ricky* pulled the trigger. Even after all this time, you never get over the pain," she says. "My heart aches for my son as much today as it did when that policeman told me what he had done. There is not a day of my life that I don't miss him—that I don't long to touch him...see him smile...to hear him say *'Hi, Mom!'*

"Whatever the reason, Ricky's gone. It won't do any good to dwell on the why or the what-might-have-been.... What is, *is*. I thank God that I had my son for twenty-two years. And I thank the Lord for giving me peace. I have asked Him to give me the strength *not* to think of that horrible day, and in His mercy, I seldom do anymore. If I find myself thinking about it, I just ask God to intervene in my thoughts...to replace them with thoughts that are pleasing to Him. That's when I start to think of the *good* things...like the way Ricky used to make me Valentine and Birthday cards even when he could afford to buy them at the store because he knew I liked them home-made. And the way he used to give me a kiss on the cheek sometimes, even if his friends would see...

"Later, people were talking about what I said when I heard about my son. Some people said I was out of my mind, but I wasn't; I knew exactly what I was saying. When something bad happens we have to choose how we're going to react. Even at that worst moment of my life, I was still a Christian. It seems unthinkable now, but I was aware of those unsaved people in my office and in spite of that tragic moment in time, the Holy Spirit enabled me to speak words meant to glorify God. *I* didn't choose those words; the Holy Spirit did.

"In the months after the funeral, there were plenty of times when I questioned God. When a tragedy hits you, it's abnormal *not* to question; God knows we're waiting to hear from Him when we ask. The *bigger* question is: How do we respond to the answer He gives? Do we tell Him He's wrong—that He didn't know what He was doing? Do we tell the Almighty God that He's *unfair?* What if we ask and He never lets us know the answer?"

She pauses, considering her own question. Then Bella shrugs her shoulders and says, "I think it's wrong to spend too much time questioning God. It's better to look at Jesus and think about how He *chose* to suffer for us. That's much more constructive."

Of all the testimonies I have heard in my Christian life, Bella's has had a most profound affect on me. Not because she is more courageous than others, and not because she has suffered more, but because her testimony is so sweetly simple: Bella seems to say: *He is my God and I love Him. He knows what is best. Period!*

Suffering is necessary if we want to be conformed to the image of Christ. Suffering refines us, and proves our faith genuine as we persevere by giving praise, glory and honor to God during times of adversity. Suffering, more than anything else, is a rein God uses to pull us closer to Himself.

Who's To Blame?

Certainly man brings much pain and suffering upon himself. In his fallen nature, man is disobedient and unfaithful to God, rebellious in all his ways. We are sometimes companions to fools, and participants in sin.

We tend to idolize money, and we're guilty of all kinds of sexual immorality and perversion. We slander our neighbor; we cheat and we lie. Then, we justify it all with phrases like: "What's the big deal? *Everybody* does it!" Or, "It was only a *little* lie; who's gonna know?" "Who's gonna get hurt?" The fact is, someone *always* gets hurt when we sin; that's why God named disobedience "sin." Often we cause our own suffering by the things we do, and at times we selfishly inflict pain on others. Is it any wonder that God sometimes deals harshly with us?

However, it would be wrong to believe that we are always the cause of our own adversity. Remember Job? He is described as a man "blameless" in God's sight, yet God allowed him to suffer tremendous pain and grief. Rabbis have been taught to believe that all suffering is God's punishment for sin. If you hurt (they've been taught), you *have* to be a sinner. They even believed that babies could sin in the womb and thus, be born defective. In addition, Jews believed that some people were afflicted because of the sins of their parents, but Jesus adamantly refuted this belief. In John, chapter nine, the disciples question Jesus about a blind man: They are certain his blindness is the result of sin. Since he had been born blind, they reasoned that he was suffering because of some horrible thing his parents had done. When they asked Jesus, *"Rabbi, who sinned, this man or his parents...?"* Jesus quickly answered, *"Neither this man nor his parents sinned...this happened so that the work of God might be displayed in his life."* (v.2-3)

Again, in Luke thirteen, some people were reporting to Jesus that human blood was sacrificed in the temple, under the reign of Pilate. They insinuated that the Galileans must have done some unthinkable thing which led to their violent demise. Jesus answers by saying, *"Do you think that these Galileans were worse sinners than all the other Galileans because they suffered this way?"*

The fact is, death comes to everyone, the righteous and the unrighteous. The *manner* of death is inconsequential. The only thing that really matters at that time is where one will spend eternity. In truth, one doesn't have to be "a certain kind of person" to suffer, and there isn't necessarily

always someone to blame. Adversity puts everyone on common ground, regardless of social or economic status. We all suffer, and we must all admit dependence upon Jesus Christ if we are going to persevere through it. Sometimes suffering is allowed just so that others can see God displayed in *our* lives.

Because Christ Suffered

To this you were called, because Christ suffered for you, leaving you an example, that you should follow in his steps."
1 Peter 2:21 (NIV)

For even hereunto were ye called: because Christ also suffered for us, leaving us an example, that ye should follow his steps.
(KJV)

Within this verse lies the basic instruction for glorifying God in the midst of adversity: No matter how bad things get, we are called to imitate Jesus Christ—to "follow in his steps." Simply put, we're to ask ourselves, *"What would Jesus do?"* and then we're called to do it!

When circumstances were the worst, Jesus stayed in close communion with the Heavenly Father. He was constantly on His knees, asking for guidance and praying for the will of His Father, in spite of the pain he would be called to suffer. Jesus didn't complain when He hurt. He didn't grumble against God, and He certainly didn't quit (Hebrews 12:3). Jesus Christ ran the race full speed. All the way to the cross.

If we are going to glorify God by imitating Christ, we have to study His life diligently so we can know Him intimately. Can you imagine someone trying to create an accurate impression of someone else, without carefully studying the person they're attempting to imitate? Just as entertainers spend countless hours studying the movements and mannerisms of their subjects before they do imitations of them, we have to devote ourselves to a study of Christ and strive to know Jesus so intimately that we know exactly how He would react if He were standing in our shoes.

Lest you feel it's hopeless, thinking *you* could *never* be like Jesus, let me remind you that just as you were born of the flesh and have characteristics of both your biological parents, you were given the heart of Christ when you were reborn spiritually into the Kingdom of God. If the desire of your heart is to imitate Christ, His Spirit will allow you to do it. As you continue to persevere in imitating Jesus during difficult times, be assured that *God will never use adversity to break a believer!* On the contrary, Jesus will mend what the world has left for broken.

No temptation has seized you except what is common to man. And God is faithful; he will not let you be tempted beyond what you can bear. But when you are tempted, he will also provide a way out so that you can stand up under it.
1 Corinthians 10:13 (NIV)

There hath no temptation taken you but such as is common to man: but God is faithful, who will not suffer you to be tempted above that ye are able; but will with the temptation also make a way to escape, that ye may be able to bear it.
(KJV)

Life Application: Chapter Four

Day One:
Read 1 Peter 1:6-9 and record your thoughts about suffering.

What do you think Peter means when he says that testing proves our faith to be "genuine"? (v.7)

What, according to Peter, is the "goal of faith" or the reward for perseverance? (v.9)

Read Colossians 3:5-10 and 1 John 2:6. Based on these scriptures and your personal knowledge of Jesus Christ, how would you compare the walk of the believer with the walk of Christ?

Day Two:
Read Luke 22:41-42. When Jesus was suffering the most painful test of His life, how did He pray?

What is the command issued to all believers in Ephesians 5:1?

When you are suffering, what should the prayer of *your* heart be?

How could you benefit from praying for God's will during adversity?

Day Three:

Using the following verses for reference, list some ways in which we bring adversity upon ourselves:

Numbers 14:33

Jeremiah 9:7-8

Psalm 107:17

Proverbs 13:20

Mark 7:21-22

Day Four:
Read 1 Peter 2:21. List some specific ways in which you can imitate Christ during difficult times:

Who is the first person you go to when you are having a crisis?

Why?

Carefully consider the words in Psalm 43:3-5. Where is the wisest, most dependable counsel found?

Why?

Day Five:

Re-read each verse printed in italics in Chapter Four and record the most significant thing you learned this week. Discuss your answer with your group.

Chapter 5

Battle Fatigue

"Let us hold unswervingly to the hope
we profess, for he who promised is
faithful."   **Hebrews 10:23 (NIV)**

When adversity continues for extreme lengths of time, the human body can grow physically and emotionally weary. Sometimes, we just grow weary of *waiting*. Though it's true that weariness may signal a lack of trust in God, it can also signify simple physical exhaustion. Two things will sustain us throughout times of weariness: A mind fixed on the Person of Jesus Christ, and a heart that never loses hope in the promise of salvation.

My comfort in my suffering is this: Your promise preserves my life.... I remember your ancient laws, O Lord, and I find comfort in them.... In the night I remember your name, O Lord, and I will keep your law.... You are my portion, O Lord; I have promised to obey your words. I have sought your face with all my heart; be gracious to me according to your promise.
Psalm 119:50, 52, 55, 57-58 (NIV)

This is my comfort in my affliction: for thy word hath quickened me. I remembered thy judgments of old, O Lord; and have comforted myself. I have remembered thy name O Lord, in the night, and have kept thy law. Thou art my portion, O Lord: I have said that I would keep thy words. I entreated thy favour with my whole heart: be merciful unto me according to thy word.
(KJV)

Is It Wrong to Grow Weary?

Feelings of guilt often accompany feelings of weariness. *"If I really trusted God, I wouldn't feel so let down."* Or, *"If I really believe God's promises, why am I so frustrated?"* If you are in a right relationship with

God—spending time with Him daily, continuing to trust in Him—don't be ashamed of temporary weariness during times of extreme adversity. This is a common human malady. We will only be held responsible for our *reaction* to the weariness we feel.

Physical weariness is usually the result of persistent stress. Coping with a long-term physical illness or death requires great patience and places extreme physical demands upon us whether we're dealing with a personal health problem, or the illness of a loved one. Loss of employment or other financial setbacks will take a toll on us because mentally, we can exhaust ourselves in search of solutions. Obstinate children may remain in a state of rebellion for *years*, until we feel completely spent with concern in spite of our best efforts to commit them to a merciful Lord. And most certainly, perseverance in a difficult marriage will test the endurance of even the most steadfast believer. *Every form of adversity requires mental and physical adjustments;* we shouldn't be alarmed if we grow physically and emotionally weary. We must be quick to recognize and avoid *spiritual* weariness, which almost always manifests itself in grumbling and complaining. To complain against God is a sin. (Job 1:22)

To understand how one keeps physical weariness from becoming spiritual weariness, consider these words from Lamentations:

I remember my affliction and my wandering, the bitterness and the gall. I well remember them, and my soul is downcast within me. Yet this I call to mind and therefore I have hope: Because of the Lord's great love we are not consumed, for his compassions never fail. They are new every morning; great is your faithfulness. I say to myself, "The Lord is my portion; therefore I will wait for him."
Lamentations 3:19-23 (NIV)

Remembering mine affliction and my misery, the wormwood and the gall. My soul hath them still in remembrance, and is humbled in me. This I recall to my mind, therefore have I hope. It is of the Lord's mercies that we are not consumed, because his compassions fail not. They are new every morning: great is thy faithfulness. ***(KJV)***

The author of those verses was about as weary as one could get. Yet in the midst of remembering his afflictions with bitterness, he had the wisdom to shift his focus from his circumstances and fix his eyes firmly upon the Lord. Suddenly God's unfailing love and compassion were like honey poured over the bitter pill of adversity. Because of God's great love, the psalmist was able to bear the pain. He was able to persevere with patience "because he saw him who is invisible" (Hebrews 11:27).

As a runner who concentrates on the finish line, we must *fix our eyes on Jesus* if we're going to finish the race energized and able to use what we've learned to minister to others. Those who succumb to weariness usually do so because they become impatient waiting for God to change things. Impatience is like a weight on the back of a runner: it slows him down, and if he sinks to his knees because of it, he'll lose the race altogether.

Sometimes weariness comes from the mental exhaustion we experience when we try (and fail) to "fix" what God isn't ready to fix. For example, in spite of our efforts to change things, no one who suffers because of sin will be blessed by God until he recognizes the sin and repents. The one who squanders what God provides will not be blessed with more until he learns to view money and possessions from God's point of view. So if we are worn-out because of our own pain (or because of someone else's), our first responsibility is to *cease striving and know that He is God.* If we continue to pray, asking God to teach us, and *if we are willing to be taught, God will answer us* in His perfect time. Our job isn't to try and fix what God has allowed to be broken; our job is to maintain a close relationship with Him as we wait patiently and expectantly for Him to act.

How long, O Lord? Will you forget me forever? How long will you hide your face from me? How long must I wrestle with my thoughts and every day have sorrow in my heart?

Psalm 13:1-2 (NIV)

How long wilt thou forget me, O Lord? For ever? How long wilt thou hide thy face from me? How long shall I take counsel in my soul, having sorrow in my heart daily? How long shall mine enemy be exalted over me?

(KJV)

Plagued all day long?

Much weariness comes from wrestling with our thoughts. In Psalm 73, the psalmist, having been "plagued" all day long and "punished every morning," admits the following: "When I tried to understand all this, it was oppressive to me" (Psalm 73:16). Just thinking about his problems made him weary! Likewise, we can exhaust ourselves trying to decipher God's reasons. When we do that, we miss the peace that comes from resting in who God is, and the assurance that He can and will deliver us. We ask, "Why me, Lord?" "When will it end, Lord?" "Is it going to get worse before it gets better?" We question God because it's a natural thing for us to do, but we have no right to expect an answer.

You turn things upside down, as if the potter were thought to be like the clay! Shall what is formed say to him who formed it, "He did not make me?" Can the pot say of the potter, "He knows nothing"? *Isaiah 29:16 (NIV)*	*Surely your turning of things upside down shall be esteemed as the potter's clay: for shall the work say of him that made it, He made me not? Or shall the thing framed say of him that framed it, He had no understanding?* *(KJV)*

In verse seventeen of Psalm 73, the psalmist says that when he entered the sanctuary of God, he was given wisdom to understand. In other words, he understood as much as God revealed to him—as much as was humanly possible. (Sometimes the only thing God reveals, is that we may never understand! Nevertheless, we can relax because He is sovereign!) While in the sanctuary, *the eyes of the psalmist were fixed on God, and his thoughts were fixed on worship; he wasn't thinking about his problems!* Likewise, our understanding will come when we "enter God's sanctuary" by setting time apart to commune with Him about the things that plague us all day long. It's important to mention here, that a sanctuary is any place you are in solitude with God. You can make your favorite chair your sanctuary, or your car. You can kneel beside your bed or take a walk in the park. Sanctuary begins in the heart of man and manifests itself in undivided devotion to God.

God's Word: "No Doze" for the Tired and Weary

"Communion" means possessing and/or sharing the thoughts and feelings of another; it is the most intimate form of spiritual fellowship with God. As with any relationship, we cannot be truly intimate unless we are truly alone. *Communion with God is a discipline that must be practiced every day.* When our lives are sailing on calm waters, it is easy to become complacent. The weather is great so we just relax in our spiritual boat, lazily floating through life. We close our eyes, taking them off God, and sometimes fall asleep unaware of the massive storm clouds developing overhead. Suddenly a loud clap of thunder or a strong squall awakens us. Only then does the reality of the storm force us to get up and act–to take control of our spiritual sails in order to survive impending disaster. As with unexpected storms, adversity keeps us alert.

Every time we grow spiritually smug, adversity comes along and smacks our knuckles with a ruler. Affliction is a stern teacher, constantly reminding us to stay in close communion with God; it shakes its finger, pointing out the necessity of complete dependence upon the power of the Holy Spirit.

...let us throw off everything that hinders and the sin that so easily entangles, and let us run with perseverance the race marked out for us. Let us fix our eyes on Jesus, the author and perfecter of our faith, who for the joy set before him endured the cross, scorning its shame, and sat down at the right hand of the throne of God. Consider him, who endured such opposition from sinful men, so that you will not grow weary and lose heart. Hebrews 12:1-3 (NIV)

...let us lay aside every weight, and the sin which doth so easily beset us, and let us run with patience the race that is set before us, Looking unto Jesus the author and finisher of our faith; who for the joy that was set before him endured the cross, despising the shame, and is set down at the right hand of the throne of God. For consider him that endured such contradiction of sinners against himself, lest ye be wearied and faint in your minds.   (KJV)

Weariness can become the heavy thing that hinders us. Impatience and grumbling can become the sins that entangle us. Imagine yourself in a race: you're wearing your hundred dollar air-sole running shoes. (You even invested in a fashionable running suit!) The number "1" is pinned on the back of your shirt—symbolic, you're sure, of imminent victory! Your toes are on the starting line, and you're set to run; you're feelin' *good!* Then someone comes up behind you and places a heavy pack on your back. Inside the pack are large stones marked, "I'm tired!" "I'm impatient!" And, "I'm angry that I have to run this race!" Weariness, impatience, and grumbling are like mill stones that weigh a runner down. Such burdens must be thrown off if the runner is going to win the race. The way to rid oneself of a burden, is to lay it at the feet of Jesus, and then to trust God to do what He has promised.

The more we get to know and understand God, the more natural our desire for communion becomes. When you meet someone for the first time, you usually don't have much to say to one another. But as you visit daily, you begin to know more about each other, and a level of trust and confidence begins to grow. Before you know it, you run out of time before you run out of conversation! It's the same way with God as we grow in our relationship with Him. The more frequently we call on Him, the more opportunities He has to prove His faithfulness. As we see His faithfulness, we learn to trust Him and feel the power of His Holy Spirit, guiding us forward through adversity. When God becomes your most trusted confidant, the first One you turn to in times of desperation, you can be sure you're in a right relationship with Him.

Even if you already speak with God daily, don't make the mistake of thinking that there's nothing more He can reveal to you about Himself. *The human mind can never know everything about God.* Of the Divinity of God J.I. Packer wrote: "It is a subject so vast, that all our thoughts are lost in its immensity; so deep that our pride is drowned in its infinity.... No subject of contemplation will tend more to humble the mind, than thoughts of God... Nothing will so enlarge the intellect, nothing so magnify the whole soul of man, as a devout, earnest, *continued* investigation of the great subject of the Deity." (Emphasis mine.)[1]

Just as communion with God is a daily exercise, Scripture is the runner's daily vitamin. The substance of God's Word is essential in daily doses if one is going to maintain spiritual endurance. Man *cannot* live on bread alone, and nothing builds stamina like the Word of God!

The law of the Lord is perfect, reviving the soul.
Psalm 19:7 (NIV)

The law of the Lord is perfect, converting the soul: the testimony of the Lord is sure, making wise the simple. *(KJV)*

Life Application: Chapter Five

Day One:
How does God view complaining? Job 1:22

Read Numbers 11:1 How do you think God feels when His people complain?

How did God react as a result of the complaining of His people?

What does this verse tell you about God?

What has God taught you about yourself?

Day Two:

Read 1 Samuel 2:10. How does God deal with those who complain against Him?

Why is it a sin to complain against God?

What does God want us to do in times of suffering?
Romans 5:3-5.

Day Three:

Note that we are to rejoice *in* suffering, not *because* of it. What enables the Christian to remain joyful, in spite of adversity?

Lamentations 3:22-23

1 Peter 1:3-7

Read 2 Chronicles 20:9. What kinds of calamity can God deliver us from?

What must we do before He can deliver us?

Day Four:

Read Psalm 15:1-5. List the characteristics of one who is qualified to stand in the presence of God:

How does this make you feel?

What do you think it means to "stand in God's presence"?

Though we all fall short of the characteristics listed in Psalm 15, we still have assurance of our position before God. Read Romans 4:20-22 and explain why:

Day Five:

Read Hebrews 12:2. What is the best way to keep yourself from dwelling on your problems?

Meditate on what it would take for you to spend more time alone with God *daily*, and record your thoughts:

At what time of day would it be easiest for you to spend time alone with God?

Where is a good place for you to spend your quiet time?

What specific steps will you take to insure a few uninterrupted minutes with God? (For example, will you take your phone off the hook? Have your quiet time while the children are napping? Get up a half hour earlier, or go to bed a half hour after everyone else?)

What are some things you can do to allow more time in your day for Scripture reading and prayer? (For example: Watch less television? Talk less on the phone? Get up earlier?)

The *amount* of time one spends with God may be less important than the commitment to try. If all you can spare is five minutes each day, ask the Lord to help you *discipline yourself* to give Him five minutes. By spending time each day in God's Word, you are actively demonstrating that He is an important priority in your life. Time is our most precious commodity. When one shows reverence for God by *tithing time,* He will add minutes to your day. How much time each day will you try to spend in communion with God?

If you feel the Lord has spoken directly to you regarding prayer and Scripture reading, ask someone in your group to hold you accountable.

[1] J.I. Packer, <u>Knowing God,</u> InterVarsity Press, Downers Grove, Illinois. 1973. P.13,14.

Chapter 6

Are You There, Lord?

"For everyone who asks receives; he who seeks finds; and to him who knocks, the door will be opened."
Luke 11:10 (NIV)

During times of struggle, we sometimes wonder if God is listening. We wonder where He is. The answer is this: *He is always with us!* He is Immanuel, *"God With Us,"* so in spite of how we sometimes feel, He is *always* present, always listening, always *hearing*. This is faith, not that we feel close to God, but that we trust that He is always close to us.

Where can I go from your Spirit? Where can I flee from your presence? If I go up to the heavens, you are there; if I make my bed in the depths, you are there.
Psalm 139:7-8 (NIV)

Whither shall I go from thy spirit? Or whither shall I flee from thy presence? If I ascend up into heaven, thou art there: if I make my bed in hell, behold, thou art there.
(KJV)

A few years ago my husband was offered a job in the Midwest and we were forced to decide whether we wanted to move from Arizona, which had been our home-base for twenty-five years. Our daughter was nineteen at the time, and our son was to graduate from High School in a couple of months. *Neither* of them had *any* intention of leaving the sunny southwest for the cold midwestern winters!

We had built our home in a small community about twenty minutes north of Scottsdale. When we moved in in the early 1970s, there were only a few homes in the area. Our friends thought we were crazy to move "so far out," but we loved the peace and quiet and the vast expanse of the desert. We chose an acre of land full of mature cactus, ironwood, and palo verde trees, and situated the house so we had an incredible view of the mountains from a large picture window in the kitchen. Evenings, we enjoyed spectacular Arizona sunsets from our living room, and the lights shimmering in the city below.

Ours was a community often visited by tourists, and I was grateful that I was living there and didn't have to get back on a bus and leave. I loved our home and was content there. I would never have *chosen* to leave it.

Beyond the beauty of our surroundings, our home had *memories.* Memories of school busses and birthday parties and forts made of cast-off lumber.... Kite flying and dirt-bikes and hikes up Pinnacle Peak mountain to see the blankets of wild flowers in the Spring.... And most significant, the inches of our children's lives measured out in pencil in the kitchen doorway....

It was difficult to think of leaving all that behind. I had to force myself to remember that none of it was important; it was all temporal. But there was more to the move than simple logistics and dying to my desires. The job meant a change of course in my husband's career. He would be in the same field of work, but in a completely different position. Instead of being in the field and physically active, he would be wearing a tie and sitting behind a desk all day for the first time in his life. So when he asked me if I thought he should take the job, I really didn't know what to tell him. What if I told him to take it, and he didn't like it? What if he *hated* it? What if I told him *not* to take the job and he missed the opportunity of a lifetime? After discussing it at length for several hours, I realized that the final decision would have to be Fred's, because he would be most affected by it. I remember telling him, "all we can do is pray." *We* didn't know what to do, but *God* knew the plan He had for us. So as I waited for my husband to decide, I prayed for *God's will* for our family.

I didn't want to move, but I was confident that whatever Fred's decision, I could live with it. I was confident of that *until* he announced that he was going to take the job. Then I remember a sinking feeling as I thought of all the friends and memories I would leave behind. For several days, I fought feelings that I can only describe as "deep sadness." I wasn't *depressed* because I had committed to accept God's will. But the more I thought about the move, the less I wanted to do it. Nevertheless, our house was up for sale, and I forced myself to start packing boxes and emptying closets.

I was in one of those closets one day when God convicted me about my attitude: I had prayed for His will, and my husband had accepted the job. As often happens in such situations, Satan began sowing seeds of doubt in my mind: *You'll hate it there! It's not fair that you have to move! Tell him you changed your mind...tell him you won't go!* As I found myself closer and closer to tears, I suddenly had some insight: This was a *test*—a chance to live by faith! Immediately, I recalled the story of Abraham, who "when called to go to a place he would later receive as his inheritance, obeyed and went, even though he did not know where he was going.... For he was looking forward to the city with foundations, whose architect and builder is God (Hebrews 11:8, 10)." As the phone rang, I told myself that we were moving, and I had two choices: I could accept it graciously, or not.

I heard my husband answer the phone, and knew from his end of the conversation that it was Sal, his new boss. I was thinking, *Oh Lord, I hope this works out; I hope we're not making the biggest mistake of our lives!* At that moment I put down the shoe box I was holding, sat down on the closet floor, and asked the Lord for a sign—anything to let me know that this move was indeed *His* will. I'll never forget that moment because I had *never* asked God for a sign before, and I probably never would have, had I not just that morning read Judges 6, where Gideon asks God to put dew on the fleece as a sign that He will save Israel. The *second* I finished asking for my sign, my husband called to me: *"Hey Lynn! Sal says not to worry; the Lord is in control!"*

It was the quickest response to prayer I had ever gotten!

The move went smoothly. We bought an old, *old* house and began to fix it up because we thought that would be fun. We both like do-it-yourself projects and it was a great way to spend time together—or so we thought. What neither of us knew was that for the first six months, as

Fred acquainted himself with his new responsibilities, he would be on the road most of the time. He helped when he was home, but that was so seldom that I ended up doing most of the cleaning, wallpaper peeling, sanding and painting myself. He kept telling me to wait until he could help me, but I insisted upon getting it done; I was tired of living in the mess.

The interior of our home has thick, solid oak doors and trim, and they were all covered with *layers* of paint. Every designer color of the last seven decades was represented *somewhere* in our old house! It would have taken months to remove the paint by just sanding the wood; I had to use strong chemical strippers. I worked myself way past my physical limit, removing, refinishing and re-hanging heavy oak doors. I stripped, sanded and scraped until I *literally* (but only temporarily) lost all the feeling in my fingertips.

After we had been in our house for about two months, and during one of those days of utter physical exhaustion from over-work, I was overcome with remorse: A *"black hole day"* if there ever was one! I *longed* for my children. I *yearned* for the warm desert sun—it was *August* and I was wearing a sweatshirt! I missed my church and my favorite grocery store, and I was lonesome for my friends. I didn't know *anyone;* we hadn't socialized at all because Fred was never home. I had no friends from church because we were still trying a different one each Sunday. To put it mildly, *I was miserable!*

As I sat on the living room floor surrounded by sawdust and disassembled bookshelves, messy cans of paint and crusty brushes, I remember feeling desperately *lonely*—-a feeling I had never had before. I remember thinking *I'm all alone!* And immediately I was impressed with the words *"NO YOU AREN'T! I AM WITH YOU!"*

I did not hear the audible voice of God, but the impression was just as strong as if I had. The minute my mind registered those words, my sorrow lifted. I *wasn't* alone and I never would be—at least not in the sense that most people think of it. Jesus is *always* with us: We cannot flee from His presence! If we go up to the heavens, He is there; if we make a bed in the depths, He is there (Psalm139:7-8). *This is my life!* I thought. *This is where the Lord has chosen to put me and I should honor Him by making the most of every day. I will not complain. I will not feel sorry for myself. I will make an effort to meet people. I will get out of this house! I will thank God for all that He has provided: this house, this job, this place. God has spoken and I will listen. He knows what is best and I will trust Him.*

Making that choice to trust God set me on a course of action that I never could have dreamed. As I was alone working to fix up our house, I began listening to Christian radio for company. There was one particular program that really interested me, mostly because of the host's passion for cultural issues. Every day, she would discuss the issues of public education, abortion, homosexuality—the subjects that get us so riled up. People would call in—even some Christians—and give her serious criticism for her "radical right-wing" views. Regardless of how hateful they were, she stood *firmly* on the Word of God, and *never* compromised Scripture.

On that *black hole day,* after I had determined to take charge of my situation, I went to the phone and called the radio station. I asked to speak with the host of the show off the air, and invited her to lunch. We became friends immediately. I was interested in the radio program and she was interested in my writing career because she had always wanted to be published. After several meetings with her at which we always discussed the state of America's culture, I asked her why she thought society was in such a mess. "What's wrong with people?" I asked.

"Well," she said, "...there are two possibilities. Either they *know* what's going on and they don't care, or they don't know. That's why I do the radio show—to get the information out."

"Have you ever thought about writing a *book?*" I asked.

"I think about it all the time," she said. "There *needs* to be a book, but I can't do it. I'm a single mom and I work full time. I don't have *time* to write a book...." And then, eyes wide with her vision, she added, "... *BUT YOU DO!*"

And thus was born the idea for *Combat Ready: How to Fight the*

Culture War. I went home that afternoon, spent about three hours writing a proposal, faxed it to a publisher my friend told me would be interested, and within three days I had a signed contract. For the next three years, the research for the book consumed me; I didn't have time to be lonely. Publication of the book led to over two hundred radio and television appearances, and a second book on the Culture War titled *The Blame Game.* Shortly after that, I had my own radio program.

One of the things I had enjoyed most about my home in Arizona was hearing the bells from the tower on top of the General Store. The plaintive sound of distant bells has always given me great peace. It was not long after that *black hole day* that I was watering plants in my back yard, and I heard church bells from a few blocks away. I remember smiling to myself, thinking that was God's way of telling me that I was "home." Every time I hear church bells, God reminds me that I am right where I should be....right where He wants me. God doesn't have to do those kind "little" things for us, but He does. He doesn't have to respond to our prayers, but He does. Those bells were a signal to me from God Himself; He had *heard* my loneliness, He *knew* I was unhappy. Those bells were His sweet way of telling me that He was near. The church bells had always rung in my new neighborhood. I had just been too busy feeling sorry for myself to hear them.

Looking back, I romanticize about Arizona because I love it. My neighborhood *was* exactly as I describe it, but truth be told, I had watched my little "village" change quite a bit over the years: Today, busses still go up there, but the city has spread out to meet the village; it's not so "far out" any more. The quaint little General Store is still there, but a few years ago it was all but hidden by an ugly gas station. Now there are post-boxes on every corner, and a shopping mall where the desert used to be. But several years ago, as we faced the thought of leaving our beautiful home for the midwest—-*without our children*—I thought it was the most perfect place on earth to live. Now I know that the most perfect place to be, is wherever the Lord has you at the time. That's where He wants you and that's where you can serve Him best.

Trusting God

Because God is always with us, He sees everything. He has seen every sin we have committed, and He has seen every sin and injustice that has been done to us. He sees and allows iniquity because He is a Sovereign God who will ultimately fuse all things together for good if we love Him. Our Lord does not leave or forsake us when we are lonely or suffering, and it is a mistake to think that He does. God's Spirit is all-pervasive; we couldn't hide from Him if we wanted to. We couldn't escape Him, if we tried. Considering that fact may give new insight into sin and why it's so offensive to God: Every time we sin, we do it directly in His face. There are no words we say, no thoughts we think that escape the knowledge of God.

The Spirit of God dwells in the heart, mind and physical body of every believer. God shares in every experience we have because of His intimate presence. In His great compassion *our Lord feels what we feel.* He will never leave us or forsake us. To assume that He doesn't hear us because He doesn't fix things right away, is to call Him a liar.

So do not throw away your confidence; it will be richly rewarded. You need to persevere so that when you have done the will of God, you will receive what he has promised.
Hebrews 10:35-36 (NIV)

Cast not away therefore your confidence, which hath great recompence of reward. For ye have need of patience, that, after ye have done the will of God, ye might receive the promise. (KJV)

And I heard a loud voice from the throne saying, "Now the dwelling of God is with men, and he will live with them. They will be his people, and God himself will be with them and be their God."
Revelation 21:3 (NIV)

And I heard a great voice out of heaven saying, Behold, the tabernacle of God is with men, and he will dwell with them, and they shall be his people, and God himself shall be with them, and be their God. (KJV)

God's will is that we trust Him, regardless of how things look. To trust God is to trust in His ability to know what is right for us, in spite of how much it hurts. Trust means we feel complete assurance that God *can* and *will* rescue and restore us in His perfect time. Hebrews 6:12 offers a wonderful promise: *After* one has *patiently* persevered in doing God's will (that will being to trust in Him), he will inherit the promises which come through faith. Remembering that all earthly suffering is temporary, please read the following verses and meditate on the implications of each:

In that day they will say, "Surely this is our God; we trusted him, and he saved us. This is the Lord, we trusted in him; let us rejoice and be glad in his salvation."
Isaiah 25:9 (NIV)

And it shall be said in that day, Lo, this is our God; we have waited for him, and he will save us: this is the Lord; we have waited for him, we will be glad and rejoice in his salvation.
(KJV)

Never again will they hunger; never again will they thirst. The sun will not beat upon them, nor any scorching heat. For the Lamb at the center of the throne will be their shepherd; he will lead them to springs of living water...
Revelation 7:16-17 (NIV)

They shall hunger no more, neither thirst any more; neither shall the sun light on them, nor any heat. For the Lamb which is in the midst of the throne shall feed them, and shall lead them unto living fountains of waters: and God shall wipe away all tears from their eyes.
(KJV)

He will wipe every tear from their eyes. There will be no more death or mourning or crying or pain, for the old order of things has passed away." He who was seated on the throne said, "I am making everything new!" Then he said, "Write this down, for these words are trustworthy and true." He said to me: "It is done. I am the Alpha and the Omega, the Beginning and the End. To him who is thirsty I will give to drink without cost from the spring of the water of life. He who overcomes will inherit all this, and I will be his God and he will be my son."

Revelation 21:4-7. (NIV)

And God shall wipe away all tears from their eyes; and there shall be no more death, neither sorrow, nor crying, neither shall there be any more pain: for the former things are passed away. And he that sat upon the throne said, Behold, I make all things new. And he said unto me, Write: for these words are true and faithful. And he said unto me, It is done. I am Alpha and Omega, the beginning and the end. I will give unto him that is athirst of the fountain of the water of life freely. He that overcometh shall inherit all things; and I will be his God, and he shall be my son.

(KJV)

Unanswered Prayer?

It is difficult to find the phrase "unanswered prayer" in Scripture. On the contrary, the Bible tells us *all* prayers are answered (Luke 11:10). Sometimes we fail to recognize God's answers to prayer because He answers in a way that is different from what we wanted or expected. Think of a little boy who prayed for a train set for Christmas. The train was all he wanted, so he asked God for it. His prayer broke the hearts of his parents, because they knew they couldn't afford one. On Christmas morning, his mother asked him if he was disappointed that God didn't answer his prayer. The little boy smiled, quite content with his teddy bear, and said, "He *did* answer, Mommy; He just said, *'No!'*"

Those who know God intimately recognize His answers, even though they come disguised as something else. *The reason for prayer is not to get something from God; the reason for prayer is to achieve intimacy with Him so we can understand His good and perfect will for us.* Perhaps you have heard someone say, "I know him so well, I can tell what he's thinking; I know what he's going to say before he says it!" Now, *that* is an *intimate* friend, and that is how we should be with our Lord! Jesus prayed that all who believe would have the mind of God and apart from worship, intimacy with Him is the foremost purpose of prayer.

God is Divine, so He answers prayer according to His divine nature—not according to human desire. Sometimes our "answer" in prayer is simply the blessing we receive when we emerge with a better understanding that the thing we're praying for isn't what we need at all.

"Adversity Ahead! Proceed With Caution!"

We could really bless God if we could see the advantage in suffering as Paul did. In 2 Corinthians 6:10, the apostle describes himself as "sorrowful, yet always rejoicing; poor, yet making many people rich; having nothing, and yet possessing everything."

We already know what we *shouldn't* do during adversity: We shouldn't grumble or complain. Now we need to look at what we *should* do: Paul instructs us in Romans 5:3 to *rejoice in all circumstances,* and he set the ultimate example for us to follow. As he was facing death, he wrote the following words to Timothy:

...keep your head in all situations, endure hardship, do the work of an evangelist, discharge all the duties of your ministry.
2 Timothy 4:5 (NIV)

But watch thou in all things, endure afflictions, do the work of an evangelist, make full proof of thy ministry.
(KJV)

The apostle Peter says something similar:

So then, those who suffer according to God's will should commit themselves to their faithful Creator and continue to do good.	*Wherefore let them that suffer according to the will of God commit the keeping of their soul to him in well doing, as unto a faithful Creator.*
1 Peter 4:19 (NIV)	*(KJV)*

In reading the above verses, we can note very specific instructions:
1) Keep your head: *Don't panic; God is near!*
2) Endure hardship: *Keep going!*
3) Do the work of an evangelist: *Praise God by telling of His good news!*
4) Discharge all the duties of your ministry: Serve others!
5) *Commit yourself to God: It's His problem; He can fix it!*
6) *Continue to do good: Stay right with God!*

Life Application: Chapter Six

Day One:

Read Matthew 1:23. What does the Name, *Immanuel* mean?

One of God's attributes is *omnipresence:* the ability to be everywhere simultaneously. Read the following verses and record what each says about the omnipresence of God:

Deuteronomy 31:6

1 Kings 8:27

Jeremiah 23:24

Hebrews 13:5

Day Two:

Read Leviticus 26:14-31 and record all that God says he will do to those who choose to disobey His Law:

Why is it necessary for God to punish disobedience?

Day Three:

Read John 9:31 and John 16:8-9. What do these verses mean to you?

List some things we can do to insure that God will "listen" to our prayers:

Day Four:

Read the following verses and note the ways in which God reacts to the affliction of the believer:

Psalm 18:17

Psalm 22:24

Psalm 56:8-9

Psalm 119:50

1 Peter 5:10

Day Five:

Read the following verses and note what God wants the believer to do while waiting for deliverance:

Psalm 4:4-5

Psalm 5:3

Psalm 7:17

Psalm 139:23-24

Acts 3:19

In view of what you have learned, what changes/adjustments do you think you should make in your attitude?

What action will you take to insure the change/adjustment?

Chapter 7

Patience
With Those We Love

"Here is a trustworthy saying that de-
serves full acceptance: Christ Jesus
came into the world to save sinners—
of whom I am the worst. But for that
very reason I was shown mercy so that
in me, the worst of sinners, Christ Jesus
might display his unlimited patience as
an example for those who would be-
lieve on him and receive eternal life."
1 Timothy 1:15-16 (NIV)

Laura and John were happily married. Quick to give parties and first on everyone else's guest list, their relationship was the envy of all who knew them. During twelve years of marriage, there had scarcely been a word of disagreement between them; arguments were almost always averted as each acquiesced to the desires of the other. From all outward appearances, Laura and John had everything: A great marriage, healthy children, a beautiful home, and social standing in their community. Then suddenly, her world fell apart.

"I guess it was middle-age crazy," Laura said. "Suddenly John didn't want to be responsible or accountable to anyone anymore. He thought only about himself. It wasn't John and me anymore, it was just John—-*his* needs, *his* desires...."

"When I found out there were other women, I was devastated. First, I went through a stage of denial—I refused to believe that John was ca-pable of doing something so *awful*. When the denial ended, I felt guilty, thinking that if I'd been a better wife, more supportive, maybe it wouldn't have happened. I began to blame myself! I mean, John was such a great guy... It *had* to be my fault!

"John promised me it would never happen again. I wanted to believe him, but I couldn't. All the trust was gone. No matter what he said, I knew things would never be the same again.

"I went into a deep depression. Feelings of betrayal and self-hate took over, consuming all my energy. I could barely find the strength to dress myself in the morning because I couldn't stand the thought of living another day with my life in such a mess. I even thought about killing myself."

She looks up, her eyes glazed with tears, but she doesn't cry. "As a child, my dad always told me I was worthless. I spent my whole life trying to prove him wrong: I put myself through college, and I had a great career before I met John. For twelve years I managed to raise two great kids and run our big house and all of our personal affairs. Now my marriage seemed such a failure in my eyes, that it convinced me my dad was right all along.

"My depression lasted almost six months, but gradually, I began to see the truth: *I* hadn't done anything wrong! This *wasn't* my fault! When the guilt stage was finally over, I got angry. *Really* angry: *How could he do this? How could he jeopardize all that we had?* When I was emotionally able, I asked John to see a marriage counselor with me. When he refused, I began to think about divorce. I didn't want that, but I figured if he didn't care enough about the marriage to try to work things out, we'd never make it anyway. When he realized I was serious about a divorce, he relented and we went to see someone.

"I remember feeling overwhelmed as I listened to John tell the counselor what a great wife and mother I was, how pretty and smart I was, how proud he was of me. No one had ever said those things to me before. For weeks afterward, his words nourished me, until I began to feel emotionally strong again. We saw the counselor four more times before John left town on an extended business trip. When he got back, things were so good between us, that we never went back. For two years life was like a second honeymoon. For two whole years I almost forgot it ever happened. "Then something occurred that made me think he might be going out again. When I confronted him, he adamantly denied it. I wanted to believe him, but I didn't want to be a fool, either. I tried to dismiss it, but it was all I ever thought about. I realized once again that all the trust was gone.

"When he was out of town, I seldom slept at all. When I did sleep, I'd dream that he was leaving me, and I'd wake up emotionally exhausted. Slowly I began to resent him for causing me so much worry. The resentment grew so deep that I began to consider ways to get out of the relationship. I felt anxious all the time.

"Just when I needed it most, a neighbor began to share Christ with me. She persisted in inviting me to a Bible study until I finally agreed to go, just to get it over with." Laura paused in her story and smiled. "Now, I *teach* Bible studies!

"Anyway, I was so emotionally starved that I asked Jesus into my heart immediately. And as I began to learn about God's forgiveness, I realized that no matter what John had done, God loved him anyway. I'd committed plenty of sins myself, and when I asked Christ into my life, God forgave them all. Now He was showing me that I had to forgive John."

Laura recalled a crucial principle of Christian faith as she continued. "I knew John had to see Christ in me if he was ever going to see Christ for himself. God changed my heart, and enabled me to forgive my husband. Almost immediately my burden was lifted, and I felt like a new person! Suddenly I realized that all the worrying in the world wouldn't change things; only *God* could change things. I made a decision to stop worrying, and start praying. I prayed for John's salvation, and because I'm a realist, I prayed that if John was continuing in this sin God would reveal it to me. At the same time, I asked for a sense of peace if everything was okay, so I could forget about the past and get on with my life. I gave everything to the Lord, because I knew *absolutely* that God would work things out (Romans 8:28). Once I did that, God gave me the assurance that even if John's infidelity continued, I was strong enough in the Lord to make it without him.

"John and I celebrated our twenty-fifth wedding anniversary last fall, and I haven't lost a night's sleep over this since I prayed that prayer. I feel peace that John has remained faithful, and our relationship is stronger than ever. Some find it hard to believe, but my peace comes from my assurance that no matter what happens, God is in control, and nothing can change the fact that Jesus is–and always will be my Husband, my · Comforter, and the Sustainer of my life.

"The best part of the whole story is that gradually—*because God gave me the faith to believe in His power*—I was able to survive an almost unbearable circumstance. I was able to live in the power of the Holy Spirit—not just read about it. By the grace of God and because of my desire for John to see Jesus in me, my husband gradually came to believe, too. Today, he's a Christian!"

Laura's story is an example for all believers who may subconsciously have grown apathetic toward God's power: As one newly experiencing the joy of her salvation, Laura depended totally upon the Lord to intervene. As she continued to pray and read Scripture daily, she was increasingly amazed at God's awesome power in her life. She knew that in the flesh, she could never forgive what her husband had done. But in the power of God's Holy Spirit, she was more than able.

Laura's marriage survived when many others would have failed because by the grace of God, she was given the ability to forgive her husband's failure. Whether your struggle is with your marriage, your neighbor, your boss or your mother-in-law, one thing is certain: *Without complete forgiveness, no relationship can be restored in the eyes of God.* Without unconditional love, no relationship can endure.

God loves *all* of His creation, no strings attached. Though we continue to sin, He continues to love us unconditionally, and commands us to love each other in the same way. In Matthew 5, Jesus is teaching the multitudes, speaking of their relationships with one another. He says: *"...if you are offering your gift at the altar and remember that your brother has something against you, leave your gift...go first and be reconciled to your brother; then come and offer your gift."* (v.23-24) Jesus exhorts believers to take the initiative in restoring relationships. He considers this so important that he encourages us to interrupt our worship and take care of the business of loving one another first.

Unconditional Love

Though we all want to be forgiven, it's often difficult for us to forgive others because the world tells us we can measure sin: *"His sin was worse than mine." Or, "Sure, I've sinned a little, but I've never done anything bad enough to deserve this!"* The truth is, there is no degree to sin. At it's core, all sin is the same because *all sin is disobedience.*

"You have heard that it was said to the people long ago, 'Do not murder, and anyone who murders will be subject to judgment.' But I tell you that anyone who is angry with his brother will be subject to judgment. Again, anyone who says to his brother 'Raca,' [an Aramaic term of contempt] is answerable to the Sanhedrin. But anyone who says, 'You fool!' will be in danger of the fire of hell."
Matthew 5:21-22 (NIV)

Ye have heard that it was said by them of old time, Thou shalt not kill; and whosoever shall kill shall be in danger of the judgment: But I say unto you, That whosoever is angry with his brother without a cause shall be in danger of the judgment: and whosoever shall say to his brother, Raca, shall be in danger of the council: but whosoever shall say, Thou fool, shall be in danger of hell fire.
(KJV)

In this passage, Jesus is saying that anger is equal to murder because murder *begins* with anger. There is also a warning in these verses to be cautious about the names we call others and the way we judge them, because holding another in contempt devalues what God has made. To harbor anger toward another of God's creation is to disobey His commandment to love one another. As followers of Christ we are called to hold all human life in the highest esteem. Regardless of the situation, we must deal with discord by showing Christ's love and acceptance. We are *all* the worst of sinners, but God has shown us mercy in spite of ourselves, and we are called to do the same for others. Christians are commanded to forgive, and called to ask for forgiveness *even if they didn't do anything wrong* because to continue in a broken relationship with one of God's children, is to exist in a broken relationship with God. Forgiveness should be equated with Christians, just as healing is equated with physicians. The act should be so closely associated with the person, that one cannot be mentioned without thinking of the other. After faith in Christ, forgiveness is the thing that most distinguishes true Christianity and sets the believer apart from others.

Remember Their Sin No More

God's forgiveness is complete and final; it doesn't mean that one day He is in a good mood about us, and the next day He is angry all over again. True forgiveness—the kind that results from a right relationship with God, doesn't continue to recall the sin and doesn't remind everyone of another's transgressions. James warns that to criticize or speak evil of each other is to fight against God's laws of loving one another. Genuine forgiveness doesn't harbor bitterness and resentment, but recognizes God's love and acceptance of the sinner in spite of the sin. When God forgives, *He promises to remember our sin no more.* When God's children forgive, they are called to the same promise.

It is very likely that everyone reading this has a relationship in their life that requires a great deal of patience. Maybe it is a disagreeable parent or a sister-in-law who constantly criticizes. Maybe it is a neighbor who tells lies about you, or a disloyal friend who has stabbed you in the back. It could be something as stressful as a co-worker who's trying to sabotage your job, or something as trivial as a husband who refuses to hit the hamper with his socks. Everyone, to some degree, struggles with relationships. Perhaps you are suffering in a relationship you feel can never be restored because the hurt goes too deep: a victim of a violent crime or physical abuse, an incest victim or one who was emotionally and physically beaten as a child. Regardless of your individual situation, God's desire is that we love *everyone,* and that includes our enemies.

"*You have heard that it was said, 'Love your neighbor and hate your enemy.' But I tell you: Love your enemies and pray for those who persecute you...*"
                    Matthew 5:43-44 (NIV)

Ye have heard that it hath been said, Thou shalt love thy neighbour, and hate thine enemy. But I say unto you, Love your enemies, bless them that curse you, do good to them that hate you, and pray for them which despitefully use you, and persecute you. (KJV)

God *graciously* gives *immediate* and *unconditional* forgiveness to all who ask Him for it. His Spirit will empower us to do the same if we desire to do His will.

Unfortunately in some relationships there are those who refuse to forgive, and others who refuse to be forgiven. Though Christians are commanded to pray *sincerely* for those who persecute them, we may come in contact with someone who won't forgive or be forgiven, regardless of how we pray. It is important to remember that we are called to make the effort, but we are not responsible for the outcome. As much as we'd like to, we cannot change the heart of another individual; only God can do that.

Divine Intervention

God intervenes in our hearts and in the hearts of others on our behalf; He changes hearts to accomplish His purpose and enables us to love the unlovable as Christ does. If you are in a broken relationship and have never prayed specifically for God to change your heart toward someone (or for Him to change another's heart toward you), you are missing out on a special blessing. Ken is a good example: Ken became a Christian as an adult. For several years following his commitment to Christ, he remained unable to face his father without fear and anger because he was unable to let go of the burden of years of emotional and physical abuse.

"Holidays were the worst," he confessed. "I always dreaded going home, but I felt I had to. The drive took about five hours, and by the time we got there, my anxiety was unbelievable. It was always the same: everyone was uneasy, walking on egg shells afraid they'd say or do something to set Dad off. I was nervous and fretful all the time, worried about our children's behavior. When the visit was over, I'd take it out on my wife, snapping at her and the kids, sulking all the way home because my dad would make things so miserable for everyone. Finally it got so bad that my wife put her foot down. She refused to spend any more holidays with my family because it created so much emotional upheaval. My wife is not usually like that, but she was adamant about this: no more holidays with her in-laws! I can't explain the relief I felt, because her decision took all the pressure off me. My parents always claimed to love me, but they caused more pain in my life than anyone else. Once I was released from the pressure of having to be with them, I was able to look more objectively at our relationship.

"My parents are heavy drinkers, and they've always been abusive to each other and to me. My dad, especially, always seems to go out of his way to hurt me. Once, when I was about five years old, he asked me to sit on his lap. I climbed up, eager for the attention. As I sat there, he began to pinch my leg. At first, I thought he was playing, and I smiled, just happy to be so close to him. Then he pinched me harder. I wanted to be on his lap, so I stayed, even though it hurt. I sat there for the longest time, letting him pinch me until it hurt so badly I couldn't stand it anymore, and I began to cry. Then he called me a cry baby and sent me to bed without supper.

"The Bible commands us to honor our parents, but how do you honor someone who keeps you in a state of confusion and anxiety all the time? How do you honor people who can't even act *civilized* to each other? I didn't know how to deal with my parents; I was really confused.

"Then, as I thought about it, God impressed upon me the fact that I seldom prayed for my parents. For the first time, I began to see that because they aren't believers, they don't see their behavior as sin that hurts others. And because the love of Christ isn't in them, they can't possibly understand each other's needs—or my needs, either. Gradually God replaced my anger toward them with compassion. I began to wonder what had happened to *them* as children, to make them the way they are. Most important, God showed me that I *have* to forgive them for the hurt they cause me; forgiveness is His command so I have no other choice! I have to accept them the way they are, and love them in spite of themselves, because *God* loves them that way. Through prayer, I realized that there is always hope for my relationship with my parents—hope that they will accept Christ, and that one day we may be able to share the good relationship God intended us to have. That's what I pray for.

"At first, God gave me such peace, I was *certain* some remarkable thing had happened that when I saw them they would both be born again, loving each other the way God intended, *caring* for each other. I created an idea in my head of how things were going to be now that I had my prayer life all squared away. Then when I saw them, I was completely disappointed because nothing had changed. Dad was still mean, Mom was still bitter, and they fought constantly— just as they always did."

Ken sighed deeply, shrugging his shoulders. "Biblically, I'm commanded to honor them, but I am *not* commanded to suffer because of their sins! So I quit going to visit them and instead I attempt to honor my parents by writing letters and having frequent, short phone conversations with them. They are welcome to come and visit, but I won't allow them to have alcohol in the house, so they never stay more than a day or two.

"I know they may *never* change, but by God's grace, I love them anyway. It's easier to be with them now, and if there is a confrontation— and there almost always is—I know that God is with me. Knowing that gives me the strength to continue honoring my parents, even though it's not the easiest thing to do."

It is important to realize that in spite of our best efforts, some situations may never change. Unless God creates individual change, we may always be stuck with bitter parents, a grumbling uncle, or a critical relative because like it or not, they are part of the family God has given us. In that case, the thing that must change is *our attitude* toward the people doing the complaining and criticizing. As Christians, we are called to seize every opportunity to allow others to see Christ in us. Sometimes that means taking it on the cheek. That does *not* mean we must submit ourselves to unnecessary pain and suffering at the hands of the insensitive; it simply means that we are not to repay evil for evil.

To struggle with a difficult relationship is no great feat. Anyone can do that, and most of us do. To *patiently persevere* through a difficult relationship is quite another thing. Christians who persevere in the Biblical sense will turn difficult relationships into opportunities to imitate Christ. They will consider Christ's reaction to those who persecuted Him, and they will strive to emulate His behavior in their own lives. Those who rely on Christ's example will ultimately be blessed by God in spite of how things look, because God will use their pain to teach them more about Himself.

Life Application: Chapter Seven

Day One:
Read and consider Matthew 5:23-24. Why is it necessary to mend your broken relationships *before* you offer your gifts to God?

If there is a broken relationship in your life, consider that person now.... Record his or her name, if you wish.

What is God's will, regarding your relationship with that person?

Do you choose to forgive that person, as God has forgiven you?

If you agree that God's will is for you to pray for that person and ask God to bless him or her, use the space below to record your prayer. Before you write, you may want to ask the Lord to direct your thoughts: Ask Him to reveal the person's deepest need, and to give you a heart not only to *forgive*, but to *love* the one who has offended you with the love of Christ.

If you have already asked for or offered forgiveness and the relationship is still broken, have you specifically asked God to change the other person's heart toward you? If not, perhaps you'd like to record that prayer in the space below:

Why do you think it is so difficult for us to ask for forgiveness?

Day Two:
Read Exodus 3:21 and Deuteronomy 2:30. What do those verses reveal about God's intervention in our relationships?

Give an example of a time when God intervened to change your heart toward someone, or to change someone else's heart toward you:

Read 1 Corinthians 9:19-24 and record what it means to you.

How could you apply the principles in 1 Corinthians 9:19-24 to your personal situation?

Day Three:

Read 1 John 2:4 and 1 John 3:6. What do these verses say about those who continue to sin?

How could this knowledge help you to persevere in a difficult relationship?

What is your responsibility to the believer committing sin?

What is your responsibility to the *un*believer committing sin?

Read 1 John 2:6. What separates believers from non-believers?

Day Four:
Read the following verses and record the directive each gives regarding how we should respond to difficult people in our lives:

1 Corinthians 4:12

Ephesians 4:12-13

1 Thessalonians 5:14-16

If you agree that God's way of handling difficult relationships is best, record the changes you will make in your behavior toward a difficult person in your life:

What will you do if the person has no interest in restoring the relationship?

Day Five:

Read 1 Chronicles 28:9. What should be our primary motivation for mending broken relationships?

Read and meditate upon Ezekiel 36:26. Given the promise in this verse, explain why it is possible for God to empower you to love the unlovable person in your life:

Record at least one new truth you learned about relationships, and explain how you plan to apply that truth to your life:

Chapter 8

Patience
In Difficult Relationships

We have confidence in the Lord that
you are doing and will continue to do
the things we command. May the
Lord direct your hearts into God's
love and Christ's perseverance.
2 Thessalonians 3:4-5 (NIV)

Relationships with unbelievers can be difficult because unbelievers do not think as Christians do. In fact, the message of the cross is "foolishness" to the unsaved (1 Corinthians 1:18) because they do not understand the things of God. Unbelievers *"have seen many things, but have paid no attention;"* their *"ears are open,"* but they *"hear nothing"* (Isaiah 42:20 NIV). For various reasons, there are those who do not desire to have a personal relationship with Jesus Christ. Such people *know* that God exists but they choose neither to glorifiy Him, nor give Him thanks (Romans 1:20-21). Nevertheless, Christians are called to be kind to *everyone* because we may be the only imitation of Christ they see.

And the Lord's servant must not quarrel; instead, he must be kind to everyone, able to teach, not resentful. Those who oppose him he must gently instruct, in the hope that God will grant them repentance leading them to a knowledge of the truth, and that they will come to their senses and escape

And the servant of the Lord must not strive; but be gentle unto all men, apt to teach, patient, In meekness instructing those that oppose themselves; if God peradventure will give them repentance to the acknowledging of the truth; And that they may recover themselves out of the snare

from the trap of the devil, who has taken them captive to do his will.
2 Timothy 2:24-26 (NIV)

of the devil, who are taken captive by him at his will.
(KJV)

Sin is always an attempt to fill a deeper emotional need, and there is no sin greater than the sin of rejecting Christ. Ironically, the One the unbeliever rejects is the only One who can satisfy the deep emotional need he has. Knowing this, Jesus ministered in the midst of sinners, stating clearly that it is the sick who are in greatest need of a physician. He did many miracles in the presence of sinners *because* of their unbelief. In much the same way, the apostle Paul, in his desire to identify with all men, said: *"I have become all things to all men so that by all possible means, I might save some."*

In his attempt to reach all people with the Gospel, Paul took some bold steps, often going out on a limb in his effort to share the truth. As disciples of Christ, we are called to do the same thing, always balancing the desire to "become all things to all men" with prudence. It can be especially difficult to have patience in relationships with unbelievers. Because of the vast difference in moral values between Christians and non-believers, we are often at odds over moral issues and that causes problems—especially within families. In such relationships, we are called to respond with *gentleness* and *respect,* but we *are* called to respond. The following Scripture was written to believers who have fallen away, but it refers to our responsibility to non-believers as well:

"Remember this: Whoever turns a sinner from the error of his way will save him from death and cover over a multitude of sins."
James 5:20 (NIV)

Let him know, that he which converteth the sinner from the error of his way shall save a soul from death, and shall hide a multitude of sins. *(KJV)*

Be wise in the way you act toward outsiders; make the most of every opportunity. Let your conversation be always full of grace, seasoned with salt, so that you may

Walk in wisdom toward them that are without, redeeming the time. Let your speech be always with grace, seasoned with salt, that ye may know how ye ought to answer

know how to answer everyone.
Colossians 4:5-6 (NIV)

every man.
(KJV)

Let your gentleness be evident to all.
Philippians 4:5 (NIV)

Let your moderation be known unto all men. The Lord is at hand.
(KJV)

Whatever happens, conduct your-selves in a manner worthy of the gospel of Christ. Then, whether I come and see you or only hear about you in my absence, I will know that you stand firm in one spirit, contending as one man for the faith of the gospel.
Philippians 1:27 (NIV)

Only let your conversation be as it becometh the gospel of Christ: that whether I come and see you, or else be absent, I may hear of your affairs, that ye stand fast in one spirit, with one mind striving together for the faith of the gos-pel.
(KJV)

Do everything without complain-ing or arguing, so that you may become blameless and pure, chil-dren of God without fault in a crooked and depraved generation, in which you shine like stars in the universe.
Philippians 2:14-15 (NIV)

Do all things without murmutings or disputings: That ye may be blameless and harmless, the sons of God, without rebuke, in the midst of a crooked and perverse nation, among whom ye shine as lights in the world.
(KJV)

Finally, brothers, whatever is true, whatever is noble, whatever is right, whatever is pure, whatever is lovely, whatever is admirable—if anything is excellent or praise-worthy—think about such things.
Philippians 4:8 (NIV)

Finally, brethren, whatsoever things are true, whatsoever things are honest, whatsoever things are just, whatsoever things are pure, whatsoever things are lovely, whatsoever things are of good re-port; if there be any virtue, and if there be any praise, think on these things.
(KJV)

The preceding verses could be summarized as follows: "Be an example of Christ in all situations. *Never* speak rudely because if your speech is gracious and godly, you will not offend anyone. Regardless of what people say to you, *never* forget that you are a Christian—an imitator of Christ. No matter how uncomfortable things get, *don't complain*. That way, no one has cause to speak badly of you or of Christ, whom you represent. The love of Christ is meant to shine through you, that you may bring His light to those who walk in darkness; your unselfish concern for all of God's creation should be evident to all who know you. Don't dwell on the faults of others. Fill your mind with thoughts that are pure and right and you will not be tempted by the ways of unbelievers."

The Company of Fools?

In addition to being husband and wife, Wayne and Jeanie were best friends. They enjoyed hiking and mountain biking and shared like interests in music and literature. They were both bright, professionally successful and sharp-witted. Laughter contributed to the success of their marriage as they managed to find humor in some of life's most trying circumstances. About two years after they were married, Jeanie became a Christian. Though Wayne was open and receptive to the Gospel, he was not a believer.

"As soon as I became a Christian, I told Wayne. I'm sure he thought it was a temporary commitment," Jeanie said, smiling. "Within a few months, we began to have problems because I told him I felt uncomfortable around our friends. They all drank too much and some of them used other drugs. Foul language and crass jokes were the norm. None of that bothered me before because I used to do the same things. But once the Lord began to change me, I didn't see any value in those relationships because I thought there was nothing spiritual to be gained from them.

"God gave me the wisdom to know that change wouldn't happen over night; we'd have to break away from the old crowd slowly or Wayne would think I was a real radical and that would *definitely* turn him off. I began to pray about it, asking God to remove the people from our lives who would hinder my spiritual walk. Within a few months, He took care of everything. First, one couple who was really degenerate moved to another state. Then a good friend of ours who had a terrible drug problem was arrested for possession and put into rehabilitation. One of the couples divorced and went their separate ways; we don't hear from either of them anymore. Another couple lost all their money and drastically changed their lifestyle so we never see them either. There is only one couple we still see frequently and that's Wayne's best friend Carl, and his wife Ellen.

"Carl and Ellen noticed a change in me almost immediately. I told them I'd become a Christian but I might as well have told them I'd grown a third arm because neither of them thought it was possible. They had a good laugh but refused to believe I was serious. That was four years ago. Now they *know* I'm serious!

"It's hard for me to be around them because I have to sit and listen to Carl's dirty jokes. I don't laugh at his jokes, but he tells them anyway. Ellen's okay, but she has always been way too liberal for me. I had never opposed her in the past, because I never saw issues like abortion, sexual promiscuity or homosexuality as sin before—I thought they were *choices*. Ellen and I have gotten into some really heated discussions—especially about abortion—and she is downright insulting sometimes. The thing that really irritates me is that in spite of her higher education, she has her facts wrong most of the time but no one convinces her of that, even when she sees the printed page.

"Ellen *loves* to argue morality with me. For the most part, I don't enjoy their company and it's difficult to endure the relationship. Then I remember that I prayed about our friends and God removed all of them except Carl and Ellen. Carl is *still* Wayne's best friend, and unless that changes, we will be socializing with them for a long time. Because they are still in our lives, I know the Lord wants it that way so I try to take advantage of every opportunity. After all this time, I don't *talk* about the Lord so much because I've said everything there is to say. Instead, I pray for them and hope they will *see* Christ in me. Carl is a good man and he would do anything for Wayne. He doesn't mean any harm. He just doesn't know any better. Ellen's worst problem is that she's too educated. She possesses an abundance of man's knowledge but none of God's wisdom; she's spiritually blind.

"As far as I know, there are no other Christian influences in their lives. Besides," Jeanie says, grinning, "...every time we get into a discussion about Jesus, Wayne's right there listening. Those discussions have thrown the door wide open for deeper discussions with Wayne and I feel he's very close to committing his life to the Lord."

━━━━━━➤◆◄━━━━━━

Lydia, a single woman in her early twenties, was the only member of her family to know the Lord. Lydia says that visits with her family are always marked by heavy drinking, abusive language and family quarrels which sometimes turn violent. Though it pains her deeply to associate with members of her own family, Lydia perseveres because of the opportunity she sees to make a difference in their lives.

"My niece Cheryl is living with a drug user who beats her," she says, wearily. "She has had two pregnancies with him and aborted both babies. Two years ago, Cheryl saved her brother's life when she came home and found him near death from a drug overdose. He was seventeen. Her mother—my sister—has lived with three different men since her divorce four years ago. One of them abused Cheryl sexually when she was sixteen. My sister has always been a lousy parent; she's selfish and neglectful. All three of her children have lived on the street because the guy she's with doesn't want them around."

She shakes her head incredulously. "Can you imagine kicking your own children out of the house so some guy you met in a bar can move in?

"My parents divorced when I was sixteen," she continues. "It was a relief when it finally happened. My dad could never hold a job and they were always fighting about money. My mom and stepfather fight all the time. It's rare if we get through a meal without one of them starting a fight and storming away from the table. Sometimes it starts with me— my stepfather likes to humiliate me when he's drunk— but usually they fight about my brother. He's twenty-eight and still lives with them because he's too lazy to get a job.

"I can't tell you how many times I've been tempted to walk away from my family. Then I look at them and Christ fills my heart with compassion. They're so... *lost.* Their lives seem so *hopeless!* Then by God's grace I remember that nothing is impossible for Him. I mean, I was in the same pit they're in until He saved me! Remembering that gives me hope that if I don't give up maybe one—or all of them—will be saved because of my patience.

"So I continue going to family gatherings, praying beforehand against the spiritual oppression that is always there. I ask God to guard my words and keep my temper in check as I view their behavior. I ask for opportunities to share the Lord with my family and I ask the Holy Spirit to make me sensitive to their needs as He gives me the right words to say at the right time. It's a struggle and it's almost always painful, but I know my suffering isn't in vain. God has a purpose in it and He's no fool. He gave me this family for a reason and in His wisdom He wouldn't give the task to someone who was incapable of meeting the challenge. My desire is to turn a difficult situation into one where God can be glorified.

"As I said, I used to think a lot about giving up. The easiest thing would be just to walk away, leaving them all behind. I mean, I'm *saved; my future's secure!* Why do I need this aggravation? Sometimes I think if they're foolish enough to reject Christ, they don't deserve eternal life! But the more I grow in my Christian walk, the more I see patience as a matter of *principle.* Of course, I *could* walk away but then I'd be a quitter. I want my Christianity to mean something. When I stand before the Lord, I want Him to chuckle and say, *'That was quite a test I gave you, Lydia, but you hung in there and I'm proud of you!'*

"About a year ago, I seized an opportunity to share the Gospel with my nephew and he prayed to received Christ. That never would have happened if I had quit. I had the privilege of giving him his first Bible and he took it with him when he enlisted in the Navy. Now I have the privilege of praying that he will continue to grow in his relationship with Jesus. I pray that the change in Randy's life will be significant enough that his sister and brother will notice Christ in him and want to have what Randy has— a transformed life. My sister noticed a change in him and when Randy told her what he'd done, she thanked me for caring enough to spend the time talking to him. That gave me an opportunity to tell her, once again, that Christ offers her new life too, if only she'd accept it."

Exhortation vs. Judgment

The Christian mission is to reach out to unbelievers, maintaining holiness because we represent the family of God. In other words, on whatever ground we meet the unbeliever, we are to be set apart—above reproach. For Lydia to drink to excess with her family or return insult for insult would be for her to become a fool herself. For Jeanie to laugh at Carl's crass jokes or become enmeshed in a heated argument with Ellen would be for her to encourage them to go on sinning.

As we spend time with unbelievers, we must not confuse appropriate Christian response with judgment. Judgment is the business of God; it is *not* the business of man. We're called to contend for the faith but we're not called to make moral judgments. Christ always separated the sin from the sinner and we have to do the same thing.

Sometimes God uses one person to help convict another of sin. When that happens, the one feeling convicted almost always responds by accusing the confronter of being "judgmental" when in fact, *exhortation* was the goal. There is a distinct difference between the two: judgment criticizes the past, while exhortation encourages one to look toward the future, to see past the temporary gratification of sin and look forward to the eternal reward which comes from living a godly life. Judgment grows out of an attitude of self-righteousness, while exhortation stems from Christ's compassion in the believer and the believer's deep concern for the spiritual welfare of another of God's children.

Blessed Are the Persecuted

As He attempted to teach unbelievers the truth, Jesus was called everything from a liar to a blasphemer. He was whipped, beaten and spat upon. When insults were hurled at Him, Jesus didn't retaliate. When He suffered, He made no threats. Instead, He entrusted Himself to God who judges fairly. Jesus repaid hatred with love and invested His time and effort to save those lost in sin. In the same way, we are exhorted to repay evil and insult with blessings and to encourage others to do good, regardless of their response to the Gospel. God's blessings abound to everyone but they cannot be enjoyed until one makes a conscious choice to enter into a relationship with Jesus Christ. Without benefit of a Christ-like example, the unsaved are left to imitate the world. The Christian who perseveres is often a plank, bridging the gap between the unbeliever and Jesus Christ. If we give up by lifting the plank and taking it with us when we go, the unbeliever will very likely plummet deeper into the abyss of sin.

Life Application: Chapter Eight

Day One:

Read Romans 9:17. Why did God "raise *you* up?"

Read Romans 10:9-10 and summarize what it says:

Read John 5:24 and summarize what it says:

The beauty in both of these verses is their *simplicity* in delivering the gospel message. When the message is so simple, why do you think most of us find it so *difficult* to witness?

Day Two:

What guarantees the believer the ability to share his faith with others?

2 Timothy 1:7

Luke 12:12

John 14:26

Explain how you feel when someone criticizes your faith in Jesus Christ:

Read Romans 1:16. Describe a time when you felt "ashamed" to share the gospel:

Read Acts 18:9-10. Explain how you *would* have handled the above situation, if you *truly* believed that God was with you and that no one would attack or harm you for defending Jesus Christ:

What does 2 Timothy 3:12 say about Christian persecution?

Day Three:

It is difficult to think of persecution as a positive experience but according to Scripture, there *is* benefit to be gained from it. Study the following verses and record those benefits.

1 Peter 3:14

Phil 1:12,14, 20-21

If one of your friends was imprisoned for preaching the Gospel, would his confinement make you afraid to share your faith, or would it make you bolder? Explain your answer.

Why, specifically, do you think Paul's imprisonment *encouraged* the brothers?

Day Four:

Read Philippians 1:27. What should the Christian's response to persecution always be?

What is the fate of those who reject the gospel?   2 Thessalonians 1:8-9

How does knowing that truth make you feel about unbelievers?

Read Hebrews 10:35-39, and summarize it in the space below:

How does God feel about those who give up? (v. 38)

Day Five:
Read 1 Timothy 4:16. List the reasons why is it so important to "watch your life and doctrine closely" when you are attempting to share the gospel with others

Note some of the areas in which you may fail to set a good example for unbelievers:

What will you do to enhance your chances of setting a better example in the future?

Chapter 9

Unequally Yoked?

[Love] always protects, always trusts,
always hopes, always perseveres.
1 Corinthians 13:7 (NIV)

A "yoke" is a rough beam of wood, securely tied to the necks of draft animals so they can be joined together to work as one. God forbade farmers to mix animals under the same yoke (Deuteronomy 22:10), presumably because the stronger animal would generate more pull and cause the weaker one to suffer. Likewise, 2 Corinthians 6:14 admonishes Christians not to be "yoked with unbelievers," presumably because suffering may result from the fact that "righteousness and wickedness have [nothing] in common."

Though Paul is speaking of personal and business relationships, his advice is especially important when choosing a marriage partner. Because believers and unbelievers may have little in common philosophically, such relationships can fail for many reasons. Most important, a deep relationship with an unbeliever may lead the believer into situations where he is tempted to compromise his faith, and certainly into circumstances of personal trials and unhappiness.

It is difficult to imagine that one who knows God's Word and walks with Him would marry an unbeliever. In most cases, couples become unequally yoked when one of the spouses accepts the Lord *after* marriage. That's what happened to Margie, who became a Christian as an adult.

For ten years Margie has continued to pray for her husband's salvation. Though Bill attends church with her regularly, he has not expressed a desire to turn his life over to Christ. Margie loves her husband deeply and perseveres in prayer for his salvation, but she fears they are drifting apart because Bill doesn't seem to care about the thing that is most important to her: her relationship with Christ.

"We have a good marriage; we've always been very close. But as I grow spiritually, my faith seems to be creeping in between us. I feel my relationship with Jesus threatens Bill because he doesn't understand it, and at this point he is not interested in *trying* to understand it.

"I try to be quiet, to win him without a word, as First Peter says. But that's really difficult because I have *very* strong convictions and I want so badly for him to believe. I constantly pray for opportunities and when God provides them, I tell Bill about everything the Lord is teaching me. I tell him about answered prayer or special insights God gives me into family relationships... things like that. Usually I sense boredom but once in a while I actually see a spark of interest!

"A couple of times, I thought he was right on the verge of making a solid commitment," Margie continued, "...but each time, something happened. The first time, he was burned in a business deal by a man who has no integrity—a man who sat opposite us every Monday night for two years in a Bible study. We found out he had swindled others as well."

"Bill's salvation is the foremost concern in my life right now," Margie confessed. "It's an issue that affects every aspect of our marriage. Slowly, we've developed different sets of friends. He's uncomfortable in my world and I'm often uncomfortable in his. It seems as if we have less and less in common with each other.

"We're often at odds over how to discipline the children. Things that I see as morally wrong are acceptable to Bill because he doesn't weigh his decisions using God's scale of values. Sometimes I'll forbid the kids to do certain things and Bill will overrule me. Then I have to deal with the issue of submission. Do I give in to him and allow our children to get into situations that might lead them into sin, or do I assert myself, assuming the role of spiritual leader of our home? Most of the time, I don't know *what* to do! Submission is the thing that confuses me most. When does submission become passivity? Is it *ever* biblical for the wife to assume the role of spiritual leader? And if I do that, how far does my responsibility reach?"

God's Plan for Authority

It is especially difficult for a wife who desires to obey God to assume the role of spiritual leadership in her home. The Bible clearly states that God's desire is for *man* to be "the head of" (or authority over) woman, just as Christ is the head of every man (Ephesians 5:23). Because the institution of marriage was ordained by God, He will use all believers who desire to do His will in unique ways to minister to their unbelieving spouses.

A believing wife can have great influence over her husband without assuming a role of leadership. She can serve as a wise counselor to her unbelieving husband by asking his permission to share with him God's perspective on issues of concern. In that way she is making the most of every opportunity by bringing biblical principles into everyday situations. Tracy did that, and because of her efforts, her unbelieving husband was able to see how God was working in her life:

"Lyle was having a terrible time at work with his boss," she explained. "It went on for several weeks and Lyle was really frustrated. The first few times, I just listened while he told me what was going on between them. Then he told me about something he had said to his boss. I thought Lyle used poor judgment and I told him so—delicately, of course.

"After he thought about what I said, he agreed with me. Then he asked me what *I* would have said. I wasn't prepared for a question like that, but instantly I knew it was one of those "opportunities" I was always praying for! Silently I asked God for His wisdom, and after a minute I told Lyle what I thought he should do. You see, I knew that Lyle's boss was a godly Christian man so I reminded Lyle of that. I also knew that his boss was being unfair and that God would convict him of that if Lyle handled it properly. So that's what I told Lyle. I said, *'He's a Christian man. I'm sure he doesn't realize how unfair this is. Tell him how you feel and why you feel that way and then trust God for the outcome.'* Then I told him I'd pray about his meeting.

"Lyle looked at me strangely. I don't think it ever occurred to him that I prayed for him! Anyway, he called me from work later because he couldn't wait to tell me how well the meeting went. At dinner that night, he thanked the Lord for working out the situation—something he'd *never* done before!"

Clearly the Lord used Tracy as a wise counselor for her husband. Because of his wife's encouragement and prayers, Lyle experienced the Lord's faithfulness in his life. Further, his acknowledgment of God's hand in his life gave Tracy great joy —joy which energized her, encouraging her to persevere in prayer for him.

The Titus 3 Principle

In 1 Corinthians 7:12-14, Paul advises Christians married to unbelievers to remain married to them. He goes on to say that if the family separates, the children might never come to know the Lord either. While the idea of "unequally yoked" in marriage is a deep and complicated issue, patience in such a relationship is rewarded when one heeds the advice given in God's Word. Titus, chapter three, offers solid principles:

1. *Be obedient, ready to do whatever is good.* (Titus 3:1) As believers our first allegiance is to Jesus Christ. Therefore our foremost desire should always be to do what is right in the eyes of God. When a decision is out of our control, the thing that is "good" in all situations is prayer. The prayer of a righteous child of God avails much, and God will honor the prayers of His children. We must be patient in prayer because that is a godly response to every situation. God can, and often does, change the hearts and/or circumstances of those who oppose His will.

Recently a father was discussing an argument he had with his unsaved wife concerning a ski trip their teenage son wanted to take. The father was opposed to the trip because the boy had been ignoring his curfew and he wasn't doing his homework. Further, the trip was expensive and the boy didn't want to earn any of the money to help pay for it. The wife, knowing her husband had already told the boy he couldn't go, overruled him. Not only did she give her son permission to go, she offered to pay for the whole thing!

Refusing to argue, this husband took his problem to the Lord in prayer.

About two weeks later, a disappointed teenager told his dad the ski trip had been canceled because there wasn't enough snow.

2. *Slander no one. Be peaceable, considerate and humble to all. Remember that you, too, used to be foolish and deceived* (Titus 3:2-3). "I'm a Christian today," Michael says, "...because of a guy I worked with who accepted me just as I was—and I was a real jerk! I always made fun of him because he'd go home to his wife instead of bar-hopping with the guys. He wouldn't even play softball on Sunday mornings because he wouldn't miss church! I stayed on his case constantly but he just chuckled and shrugged it off. One time he told me if I'd go to church with him *first*, he would pitch for us and we might even win a game! He tried lots of times to tell me about Jesus but I told him I didn't want anything to do with any 'holy-rollers!'

"We worked in a warehouse and everyone used to pilfer stuff—nothing big, just little stuff. Everyone, that is, except Jim, the Christian guy. Well, one day my buddy and I got caught taking some blank cassette tapes home and we both got fired. I'll never forget the look on my wife's face when I told her—we had a brand new baby at the time.

"The next day I went back to work to clean out my locker and there was Jim, waiting for me. I'm thinking he's coming over to gloat, but instead he shakes my hand, wishes me good luck, scribbles his phone number on an envelope and tells me to call him if I need anything! Well I, being the ungrateful guy that I was, threw the envelope in the trash while he watched, grabbed my stuff and walked out.

"Almost three months went by and I couldn't get work. My wife had some complications with the baby and we had lots of medical expenses and no insurance after I got fired. The pressure was too much for her and we started fighting all the time. I started going out and getting drunk. I took it all out on my wife but the truth is, I was really mad at myself—mad for goofing up like that and being so irresponsible.

"Just when things were at their worst, Jim called me up to say a friend of his was looking for a replacement on a loading dock and did I want the job? It was only a few blocks from where I used to work and it paid eight dollars a week more than I had been making. That doesn't sound like much now, but it was then, so I took the job."

He smiles. "I've been with the company twelve years; I'm a foreman now. Jim's friend—the guy who hired me—is a Christian, too, and he led me to the Lord."

Michael reconsiders, then corrects himself: "Well, Bud shared the Gospel with me, but it was really because of Jim's example that I became a Christian. That guy never said one bad thing about me—not *once*. And you know what else? No matter what I did—cussing, smoking cigarettes, drinking, goofing off at work—he never acted judgmental toward me. If it hadn't been for Jim offering me a second chance, I don't know where I'd be today. He never made me feel like he was better than me even though I can see now that he was."

To speak ill of one who does not have the light of the Gospel is to break God's command to love one another. To belittle another's judgment when he doesn't possess the wisdom of God is to belittle a child whom God loves. We were all in the same place before God saved us: we were lost in the darkness, ignorant of the Truth. God's desire is for others to see His light in us and desire to walk in it. Nothing snuffs out the light of Christ as quickly as a wind of harsh, judgmental words.

3. *Avoid foolish controversies; these are unprofitable and useless* (Titus 3:9). "I've known Merrill for nine years," Wendy says. "She is a die-hard agnostic who takes pleasure in tossing her higher education in my face. Though I continually challenge her to study the historical evidence, she maintains a *'don't confuse me with the facts'* attitude about the resurrection of Christ. She says my faith is fine for me but that those 'in academia' could *never* accept the resurrection as fact—no matter *what* the history books say!"

Such an attitude is narrow-minded and pompous, but nothing is ever gained from petty quarrels over spiritual matters. When godly wisdom is consistently met with argument, the wise Christian will not persist. Again, *the power of prayer will succeed where man's most carefully chosen words fail!*

The Attitude of Christ

Barbara and Ben had been married twelve years when Ben accepted Jesus Christ as his Lord and Savior. Swiftly and zealously transformed, Ben insisted that the whole family accompany him to church on Sundays. Reluctantly, Barbara agreed.

Every Sunday for a year Barbara tagged along, hovering in the background as Ben never missed an opportunity to point out to anyone who'd listen that his wife "wasn't saved." As Barbara stood humiliated, self-consciously watching her husband become more involved in his church and less involved with his family, she began to deeply resent his faith.

"One of our children got saved right after Ben did," she says. "The other one is like me—-not sure. I mean, I see a lot of good changes in Ben, but I don't think it's right for him to keep shoving what he believes down my throat. He has a way of making me feel *inadequate*—-like I'm not quite as good as he is because I didn't jump in with both feet just because he told me to. Since he has made all these changes, I'm trying to change, too--I really am! But if I slip up and swear, or if I want a second glass of wine, he looks at me like I've got the soul of a serial killer or something!

"Ben made a big commitment; he promised God he would try to live a certain way, to act as Jesus would in all things. That meant changing a lot of things around here! Well, I don't know if I can make the changes in my life as Ben did. I went to church as a kid. I believe in God, and I know He takes oaths seriously. I'm not about to make any promises I can't keep!"

Though people like Ben may possess knowledge of the Word of God, they have not matured enough spiritually to possess wisdom. Ben definitely has knowledge; he knows everyone needs salvation. But he doesn't have the wisdom to know that he must apply *all* of God's Word to his life if he wants to inspire a desire for Christ in the hearts of others. Godly wisdom grows from the *application* of Biblical knowledge.

Christ was a *gentle* man. He never "shoved" His truth down the throats of those He desired to save. Jesus simply presented the facts and waited for the Holy Spirit to move in the heart of the hearer. Though He was King of Kings and Lord of Lords, Jesus never allowed His position at the right hand of the Father to get in the way of His relationships with any of God's children. And neither should we. We are called to be humble in heart as Jesus was, always remembering that we did not receive eternal life because we *deserved* it. We have been saved only because of God's great love and tender mercy.

Certainly Barbara has heard God's plan of salvation. She never said she didn't believe; she only said she "wasn't sure" —a statement which indicates that she probably just needs more time to process what she's heard. Barbara never verbally rejected Christ, so Ben can't possibly know *for sure* whether or not she has. It is presumptuous for him to tell others that she has. While Ben's concern for his wife's salvation stems from his genuine love for her, spiritual intimidation seldom (if ever) has won anyone into the kingdom of God. If Ben wants to see his wife accept Christ, *he* must become more like Christ himself; he must love her unconditionally and then get out of the way and let the Holy Spirit do the work of God in her heart.

If you are a believer unequally yoked with a nonbeliever, you must stop thinking of your spouse as "unsaved" and begin to think of him or her as the partner God gave you for life. Instead of dwelling on your spouse's shortcomings and dreaming of how wonderful things will be once he or she accepts the gift of salvation, ask the Lord to fill your mind with *His* perspective on your marriage *now,* and what He wants it to be.

How can you be a better example of Christ in your marriage?

What can you do to allow your mate to *see* Christ in you?

What can you do *today* to show your spouse God's *unconditional* love?

How can you use your situation to grow in your knowledge of God?

What can *you* do to strengthen the relationship in which God has placed you?

Ask God to give you the capacity to apply His unconditional love to your relationship and He will honor your request. Forget about what *you* want for your spouse and concentrate on making your mate feel like the most important person in your life because that's what God expects you to do. Then relax and remember that the eternal life of your spouse rests not in your hands, but in God's. Trust in the knowledge that no matter how badly you long for the salvation of a loved one, no one can say "Jesus is Lord," except by the Holy Spirit.

Life Application: Chapter 9

Day One:
Read Acts 16:31. What does the verse imply to you?

Why do you think God put that verse in the Bible?

Read 1 Corinthians 12:3. Do you believe one's salvation can assure the salvation of another? Why or why not?

Day Two:
Read and paraphrase the following verses:

1 Peter 3:1-2

Philippians 4:5

Colossians 4:5-6

What do the preceding verses teach you about sharing your faith?

Day Three:
Read Isaiah 40:31. Where can the spouse yoked with an unbeliever find his/her hope and strength?

Read Lamentations 3:26. What should the unequally yoked spouse do as he/she prays for the salvation of his/her mate?

Why do you think God commands us to "wait quietly"?

Day Four:

When we want God to act on behalf of someone else, we are praying "intercessory" prayers. Intercessory prayer is the most effective weapon we have against an enemy who wants to keep our loved one blinded to the truth. To find the prerequisites for *answered* prayer, look up the following verses:

Psalm 66:18

Mark 11:22-25

John 15:7

Ephesians 6:18

Philippians 4:6

Day Five:

   Read 1 John 5:6.

   Record one new thing that the Spirit of God revealed to you this week, and share with your group how you think God wants you to apply that truth to your life:

Chapter 10

Living With Dying

If only for this life we have hope in
Christ, we are to be pitied more than
all men.
1 Corinthians 15:19 (NIV)

"Death is God's delightful way of giving us life." —Oswald Chambers

Throughout the book of Ecclesiastes, Solomon repeatedly proclaims the futility of life. "All is meaningless," he says, "...a chasing after the wind." When the physical life is over, "the dust returns to the ground it came from, and the spirit returns to God who gave it." From the day man is born, his physical body begins to deteriorate. This is the second law of thermodynamics: Everything physical proceeds toward greater loss of energy and eventual decay. While evolution is a *theory* (though often presented as fact), thermodynamics is a *law of nature* which irrefutably denies the possibility that man somehow evolved from a lower species.

As we understand that man is continually moving toward death it is good to know that physical life is nothing more than a series of tests through which one's character will be revealed for eternity. Man was created to worship God; he succeeds or fails at worship based on the way he reacts to the ordinary (and sometimes, *extra*ordinary) circumstances in his life. To praise God *in spite of* how one feels is the purest form of worship. To keep one's eyes fixed firmly on Christ in spite of physical discomfort is an effort which brings great glory to God.

Physical illness is a fact of life; if you are not suffering physically, you know someone who is. Those who think we can escape physical pain because we are children of God are forgetting that we are targets of Satan *because* of our position with Christ. To think God is unfair for allowing Christians to suffer physically is to deny His mercy and His promise to work all things together for good for those who love Him and are called according to His purpose. If one cannot understand God's reason for the physical suffering in his or someone else's life, he has not dug deeply enough into the Word of God.

The greatest danger of any illness is not the inevitability of physical death; it is the possibility of spiritual death as Satan tempts us to dwell on the pain of the natural body. Satan will persist in using our physical discomfort to keep us focused on self: *Our* discomfort, *our* misfortune, *our* pain. If the believer gives in to such deceit, he will find himself sinking deeper and deeper into the black hole of spiritual destruction until he finds himself not only physically withered but spiritually dead as well. At such times, the physically ill must remember that *all* of God's people suffer; suffering is a *privilege* granted unto us because of our relationship with Christ (1 Peter 4:12-13). None of God's children escape pain; pain only differs in kind and intensity. The desire to glorify God *in spite of* one's pain is the thing which lifts the sufferer from the pit and sets him at the feet of Christ, the Healer.

The one who patiently perseveres in faith will understand that no matter how great the pain, physical affliction is only temporary. The hope of the believer lies always in the *eternal;* regardless of our discomfort, pain cannot affect our relationship with God unless we allow it to. The thorn in Paul's flesh kept him on his knees before God. Three times he asked God to remove it, and three times God refused. But it was at this time—when Paul was presumably in extreme pain—that God taught him a most *profound* truth: *God's grace is sufficient, for His power is made perfect in our weakness* (2 Corinthians 12:9)! Just as God did not abandon Paul in his pain, He will never abandon us. Those who persevere will remember that "neither death nor life...angels or demons...present or future, nor *any powers*, neither height nor depth nor *anything else* in all creation..." (including physical pain) can separate us from the love of God that is ours in Christ Jesus, our Lord (Romans 8:39).

God is the Giver and Taker of life. He allows each of us a certain number of days to live between physical birth and death. Those days are limited and predetermined, and we will be held accountable for what we do with each of them. Days wasted in self-pity and bitterness do nothing to move us toward holiness. Days offered to God as a living sacrifice not only bring glory to the Giver of Life, they set an example and leave a strong legacy of Christian perseverance to all who observe the believer's suffering.

The one who has a right relationship with God through Jesus Christ has no need to fear death. On the contrary, he should *look forward* to death because God promises that "no eye has seen, nor ear heard, no mind can *imagine* what God has prepared for those who love Him!" (1 Corinthians 2:9) Because there is no death for those in Christ, our relationship with him prepares us to meet any physical challenge ordained for us by God. While *all* physical bodies are constantly moving toward decay, the spirit grows progressively stronger through faith that perseveres. We have no control over the physical ailments God allows in our lives, but we *do* have control regarding the way in which we respond.

Faith means "knowing *nothing...*"

Jane and Richard lost a child to cancer. Before little Janie died, they watched their daughter lead several young people to Christ from her hospital bed. When the Lord finally took Janie home, Jane and Richard rejoiced that her pain was over and she was finally at peace, in the loving arms of Jesus Christ. As their joy in the Lord outweighed their sorrow, the hospital chaplain felt certain the family was out of its mind with grief, and accused them of being in denial.

"Massive denial," Jane explained. "That's what the chaplain said. He couldn't understand that our hope was stayed on Jesus Christ, regardless of the circumstances of the moment. When I knew Janie wasn't going to get better, I reached the point where I let go of everything except Jesus. We had prayed for Janie's healing, but our *hope* was in Jesus because we knew that hope was all we could count on. Faith doesn't mean that we know God will heal. Faith is *trusting* without knowing— *anything*— apart from the certainty of our relationship to Christ.

"We are on this earth to glorify God. If that comes through suffering,

I consider my suffering a privilege and I know Janie felt the same way. When people ask me what possible good can come from the death of a child, I remember Paul, who said from prison, 'Don't feel sorry for me. While I'm here, I see progress in the Gospel.'

"Because of Janie's faith, others have come to know Jesus Christ. *Others will live for eternity because of my precious Janie!* As she lay dying, she knew God was using her and that was her joy. God's grace has allowed us to persevere in spite of our pain. I believe others have seen Christ in us and that has brought glory to God."

As Christians, we are constantly being observed. Believers and unbelievers alike will note our disposition under pressure. Christians who waiver in their faith will be discouraged by our defeat. Similarly, *nothing* disheartens an *un*believer as quickly as the words of a Christian who has taken Satan's "self-pity" bait. To give in to self-pity is to give Satan yet another weapon to use against us. If Satan convinces the believer that God is against him, the believer's attitude conveys that feeling to others and the *un*believer will see no advantage to the Christian life.

For men are not cast off by the Lord forever. Though he brings grief, he will show compassion, so great is his unfailing love. For he does not willingly bring affliction or grief to the children of men.
Lamentations 3:31-33 (NIV)

For the Lord will not cast off for ever: But though he cause grief, yet will he have compassion according to the multitude of his mercies. For he doth not afflict willingly nor grieve the children of men.
(KJV)

A mother who lost her seventeen year-old son to a drunken driver commented in her grief that, "Nothing good can ever come of this." Three days later at her son's funeral, two young people gave their lives to Christ. Today one of them is a minister.

"I can see now," this mother says, "...how God used Jeff's death to bring glory to Himself." She smiles. "For a few years after Jeff died, that thought continued to horrify me. I couldn't understand why a loving God would let a great kid like Jeff die just so He could glorify Himself. Then I thought about Jesus and I realized that God loved *His* Son just as much as I loved Jeff, yet He sacrificed Him for *me*. Because God's Son died, Jeff lives, even though his physical body is no longer here. I don't think of Jeff as dead, anymore; I think of him as absent, because that's what he is. He is absent from me, but he is present with the Lord, so the absence from me is only temporary. I still think about him every day, but now I have a more rational perspective. Now," she says with a radiant smile, "I look forward to the time when I will be reunited with my precious son in heaven—what a reunion that will be!"

Thoughtful for a moment, she sips her tea. "The peace that comes from that kind of understanding is supernatural, given by the grace of God. I could never put into words how it feels to lose a child. There aren't words in any language to describe the anguish, the pain. But when I hurt the most, God gave me new insights into the death and resurrection of Jesus Christ. When I began to concentrate on Jesus, when I began to compare Jeff's death with Christ's death on the cross, God gave me a new perspective. God's love is boundless, incomprehensible to human understanding. I think God loved His Son more than I could ever love mine because God's love is supernatural. I realized that for as long as Jesus lived, His Father *knew* that He was born to die. From the very first moment that God looked upon Him—a chubby-cheeked little baby lying in a manger—God *knew* the pain that this child He loved so much would face. Yet he offered His own Son willingly.

"Jesus was persecuted all His life. He suffered indescribable humiliation and pain..."

The mother's voice cracked as she drew a comparison in her mind, the recollection of the horrible day her son died, suddenly born afresh. She took a deep breath and wiped tears from her eyes. "The paramedics said Jeff died instantly; he didn't suffer at all. And while he was with us, he had a wonderful life. He had lots of great friends. He was a really happy kid; always smiling, always telling jokes...always telling his dad and me how much he loved us. He played sports, got good grades in school, and he was looking forward to college....

"After the funeral those two friends who committed their lives led others to Jesus. Jeff was a committed Christian himself. Only God knows how many lives he touched. I still don't understand why Jeff had to die. I don't understand a lot of the ways in which God works, but I made a choice long ago to trust Him. And the peace He's given me... well, the *peace* is unbelievable!"

Suffering, more than anything else, keeps us on our knees; perseverance and pain, blended with trust in a sovereign God Who allows all things, form the soil which cultivates strong faith.

Cheri suffered from deep depression. If she was able to sleep at all, severe anxiety would often wake her. Before she became a Christian, Cheri saw several different therapists and took various medications, but nothing could rid her of her torment. She admits that at one point she simply "ran out of trust in God," and contemplated suicide.

"I was a new Christian," she said, "...and I was attending a Bible study. My anxiety attacks were always worse the night before class and often I would be up all night. In spite of the exhaustion I felt the next morning, I'd somehow manage to drag myself to class. It was hard because I usually didn't want to go. I was angry. I mean, I'd given my life to Christ; *now I was a child of God!* I expected to be instantly free of the depression; I thought Christians weren't supposed to have problems! I was learning about God wanting the best for His children and His being merciful and all that... I just couldn't understand why the attacks continued. Well, not only did they *continue*, they got *worse!*

"But God *was* merciful and through the Bible study, I met some women who cared enough to encourage me. They took time to talk to me and they helped me see that my anxiety was nothing more than spiritual warfare—the devil wanted to keep me depressed because that way, I would feel too beaten to think about God, too depressed to want to read my Bible and too sad to feel the joy of the Lord. God talked to me through other Christians and by His grace, I *heard* what they told me, in spite of the devil's attempt to keep me deaf. I kept going to class and to worship on Sundays, but most important, I read my Bible every day. Sometimes I could only concentrate for five minutes, but I read *every day* and that wasn't easy! There were days when I had to *struggle*—literally, to open my Bible because the opposition was so strong. But I persisted. Some days I would read for a few minutes, close the Bible and not remember anything I had just read. Then later in the day I would be in the midst of a problem and the Lord would bring the Scripture to mind. As I remembered the basic truth of God's Word, I realized that the important thing was *obedience*: God commands us to know His Word. As long as we remain diligent in Bible study, God's grace will allow the Scripture to be applied to our lives.

"I've been a Christian for three years now and I've had *Christian* counseling; I know who I am *in Christ;* that's what makes the difference! Not only are my anxiety attacks almost non-existent, but now I'm training to counsel other women who are victims of abuse and depression. For the first time in my life I feel valued and necessary. My relationship with Jesus did all these things for me and not a day goes by that I don't thank God for my new life in Christ."

Faith Makes the Difference

I once attempted to comfort a young woman who suffers from a permanent, incurable disease of the nervous system. The illness causes her constant, excruciating pain; she likens the feeling to being burned with a match, twenty-four hours a day. The medication she takes affects her balance and thought process and does little to alleviate her suffering. Though she was not a Christian, she called our church because she needed to talk to someone. She was going to kill herself. She wanted to die, she said, because *anything* would be better than the quality of life which had been forced upon her by a merciless God.

Our first meeting lasted three hours. During that time, I learned that she had been engaged to be married but when her doctor diagnosed her problem, her fiancee broke off the engagement. Becoming incapable of working at twenty-five years old, she had lost her medical coverage and was forced to move in with her retired parents. Within two months the girl's bitterness and constant complaining drove both parents out of the house and they took part time jobs just to get away from her. In the evenings they went bowling, played cards or went out to a movie—anything to avoid being at home with her.

I'll never forget the sinking feeling I had sitting next to her. I prayed silently that God would give me direction; I was clearly in over my head. I'm not a trained counselor; I'm only someone who listens—a pair of ears attached to a compassionate heart. She told me of the anger she felt toward the doctor whose carelessness (she was convinced) had caused her illness. She expressed her bitterness toward a younger sister who she said, "gets everything she wants and is not nearly as good a person as I am." And she felt deserted by parents who thought she was exaggerating the pain because she'd been jilted by her boyfriend.

For at least thirty minutes, this woman attempted to describe her disease to me. She had taken photo copies of articles in medical journals and books from all over the country and filed them neatly in a three ring binder so she could read and talk about the disease. She had gone to great lengths to contact other people who shared this rare malady and though none of them lived in the same state, she spent hours on the phone every week talking to them about the illness. She even invested in a video tape which explained the disease, and had watched it so many times she could almost recite it verbatim. It became obvious to me that she was obsessed, and I suggested that her obsession only intensified her suffering. "*Maybe*," I suggested, "*...if you got out of the house...*"

She interrupted my suggestion. "I can't go out. All I can wear is loose fitting, light weight things like this," she said, pulling the night gown away from her body. "I can't have anything touching my skin; it's too painful. The doctor was going to put a morphine bag in my stomach but I didn't want that; I don't want to be more drugged up than I am, now. The pain is indescribable," she went on to say. "I can't sleep and I can't get through a day without pain pills."

She looked directly in my eyes: "There's no cure for this," she said. "I'm going to have this for the rest of my life. Do you understand why I want to die?"

I remember staring blankly at her, not knowing what to say because frankly, I don't know if *I* would want to continue living under those circumstances. But I knew she was serious about suicide because she had attempted to take her life once already. I *had* to respond in some way but it was difficult to know what to say since, from her perspective, there was no way out. From my perspective, there was *One* way out. It was obvious to me: I had to make this woman see that without Jesus Christ, she had no hope at all.

Knowing she was Jewish, I shared the Gospel message with her. As she listened intently and asked questions, I realized immediately that she had given the idea of Jesus serious thought before. For over an hour, I attempted to share my understanding of the Divine perspective on suffering. She asked questions about God's judgment because she was convinced He was punishing her for something. As God enabled me to answer her questions, I began to pray that she would make a decision to ask Christ into her life.

I talked with her for many months, several times at late hours of the evening when she couldn't sleep. Often, she would call me with questions about Jesus because she had been talking to her Rabbi. Sometimes she would want to hear (again) my opinion on why God was "making her suffer." Each conversation left me overcome with sadness for her because there was nothing I could do about her illness and nothing I could do about her lack of faith. Many times after conversations with her, I would lie awake all night, burdened with questions myself: *She's only twenty-five, God! She'll have to live in pain for a long, long, time; please be merciful and end her suffering! You could heal her, Lord, if You wanted to. Why don't You?*

It occurred to me that if everything Linda said about her disease was accurate, suffering was the *best* she could hope for; but if she would only let Jesus into her life, she would have eternity to look forward to. I continued to listen to her complaints, at the same time answering the same questions about Jesus over and over again. In all those weeks, I never saw any indication that anything I said was making an impression on her. Finally, I told her that *I* couldn't prove Jesus to her; she would have to ask *God* to reveal Him to her. A couple of days later, she called to tell me that she believed.

Though she claimed to know that Jesus was real, Linda never asked Him into her life. At least not in the time that I knew her. She never repented of her sins or trusted God to give her peace. Instead, she allowed bitterness and anger to become chains which bound her, and without the power of the Holy Spirit, she didn't have the strength to break away and move toward God.

Though she believed in the Person of Jesus and accepted him as the Messiah and the Son of God, Linda didn't have faith in the *Words* of God—Words that *promised* to rescue her from her suffering and give her new life—now and forever in the presence of the Living God. Because of her lack of faith in the promises given by God through His Word, Linda has no hope.

***

Less than twenty-four hours ago, as I sat writing this chapter, I received the tragic news that one of my dearest friends had lost her seventeen-year-old son in an automobile accident. Adam and my son had been best friends for eleven years; they played their first organized baseball game together and last Saturday, they played Adam's last. As our family stood in the midst of the mourners and grieved at the sight of Adam's teammates embracing his mother and father, we questioned God's reason over and over.

My comfort in my suffering is this: *God's promise preserves Adam's life* (Psalm 119:50). God has promised that He is merciful and that He desires no one to perish, but for all to have eternal life. He promises to comfort those who mourn and to be a stronghold to all who call upon His Name.

Man, with his finite mind, simply cannot understand the infinite ways of God. Sometimes God chooses to reveal His reasons; more often, He does not. God doesn't *owe* us any explanations because the clay dare not say to the Potter, "What have you made?"

Naked I came from my mother's womb, and naked I will depart. The Lord gave and the Lord has taken away; may the name of the Lord be praised. Job 1:21 (NIV)

...Naked came I out of my mother's womb, and naked shall I return thither: The Lord gave, and the Lord hath taken away; blessed be the name of the Lord.   (KJV)

Though it is wrong to question God, it is perfectly right to ask Him for the wisdom to understand. And it is perfectly acceptable to ask God to deliver us or anyone else from physical pain. As His children, God has given us the right to "climb into His lap" and say, *"Abba, Father; everything is possible for you. Take this cup from me."*

Though God allows physical affliction, He does not bring it willingly (Lamentations 3:31-33). He does not find joy in our suffering. As with all adversity, physical affliction is given so that God's purpose might be accomplished through us. If one desires to seek God's will and remains eager to determine His purpose, even the most excruciating pain can be used for good. To accept pain because we know we cannot change it is one thing; to accept suffering *willingly* because we know God allows it is quite another. We must continue to pray, believing that God can change things if he wants to, and understanding that if He doesn't, it is because His love and wisdom are perfect for us.

When you or someone you love is suffering physically, you must continue to pray as long as the desire for change exists, but remember that you will not experience peace in your soul until you are willing to say, *"Yet not what I will, but what you will."* Then you must *trust Him.*

If you are suffering physically, remember that God's Word stands firm, regardless of individual human experience. A committed Christian who has not suffered your pain is still able to empathize with you because the Christian who possesses the Spirit of God has received the heart of Christ along with God's promise of salvation. The Spirit-filled Christian *can* feel the pain of another and bear his burden. Counsel given in accord with God's Word can be trusted, apart from the personal experience of the counselor.

For as long as you live, you or someone you love, may have to endure physical pain. God's plan may be for you to suffer pain all your days on earth. But God promises to uphold those who are weak; He promises to carry us—to be our strength.

Even to your old age and gray hairs I am he, I am he who will sustain you. I have made you and I will carry you; I will sustain you and I will rescue you.

Isaiah 46:4 (NIV)

And even to your old age I am he; and even to hoar hairs will I carry you: I have made, and I will bear; even I will carry, and will deliver you.

(KJV)

Life Application: Chapter Ten

Day One

According to Psalm 51:12, what will sustain the believer in times of pain?

What does Exodus 4:11 say about God?

Read John 9:2-3. Why does God allow affliction in the lives of those He loves?

Consider the following situations and discuss ways in which they could be used to glorify God:

A. A child is born with a birth defect.

B. A person suffers with a chronic illness.

C. A loved one dies tragically.

Day Two:
What does Psalm 139:16 say about life span?

In view of God's Words in Psalm 139:16 and Exodus 4:11, do you think anyone really dies or is afflicted "by accident"? Explain your answer.

Read Job 1:20-22. What did Job do when he heard of the deaths of his children?

What was the result of Job's suffering? Job 42:5-6

Day Three:

Read 1 Corinthians 15:44-46. Why do you think God gives physical life before spiritual life?

Read Isaiah 43:1-3. What are the promises God makes to those who go through difficult times?

How many times does the word "when" occur in the second verse?

What does that mean to you?

Day Four:

Read Romans 4:18-20. What does the Scripture reveal about Abraham's faith?

What do you see as the "bottom line" in Abraham's faith?

What is God's command to believers regarding suffering? Revelation 2:10

How can one who suffers physically, remain faithful?

Day Five:

Read 1 Samuel 2:6 and summarize what it says:

Read Isaiah 57:1-2. Why does God allow the righteous to die?

What is the destiny of the righteous man who loses his physical life? (v.2)

Review the chapters of this book, and list the most significant things you learned about suffering:

How has this knowledge changed your spiritual life?

Blessed is the man who perseveres under trial, because when he has stood the test, he will receive the crown of life that God has promised to those who love him.

James 1:12 (NIV)

To contact Lynn Stanley, or for comments on this study or information regarding other studies in this series, please contact Focus Publishing:

Focus Publishing
1375 Washington Avenue South
Bemidji, MN 56601